Alberta/A Celebration

The Alberta Gas Trunk Line Company Limited is very proud to join in Alberta's 75th birthday celebrations with the publication of this specially commissioned book.

Alberta/A Celebration combines the talents of a distinguished author, a widely acclaimed painter-photographer, and a noted film maker. We are most pleased to present their work to the people of Alberta and to all Canadians.

As part of our own Diamond Jubilee celebrations, complimentary copies of this book are being sent to all schools, libraries, and hospitals in the province.

May we take this opportunity to wish all Albertans a happy 75th birthday and good health and prosperity for the future.

The Alberta Gas Trunk Line Company Limited

Alberta A Celebration

Stories by Rudy Wiebe
Photographs by Harry Savage
Edited by Tom Radford

Hurtig Publishers
Edmonton

Hurtig Publishers, 10560-105 Street, Edmonton, Alberta

Canadian Cataloguing in Publication Data

Wiebe, Rudy, 1934-
    Alberta, a celebration

    ISBN 0-88830-167-7

    1. Alberta–Description and Travel–Views
I. Savage, Harry   Ii. Radford, Tom, 1946-
III. Title

PS8545.I39A5   C813'.5'4   C79-091021-7
PR9199.3.W47A5

Contents

7   Foreword

12   Acknowledgement

31   The Oil Capitals of Canada

40   Lake Isle of Innisfree

43   They Just Won't Believe

65   Chinook Christmas

77   The House Smashers

99   A History of the New World

104   Growing Up in Rosebud

106   The Funny Money of 1980

131   The Angel of the Tar Sands

135   The Darkness Inside the Mountain

161   Bears, All the Time Bears

165   After Thirty Years of Marriage

195   From Montreal, 1848

197   The Year We Gave Away the Land

Dedicated to Our Parents

Foreword

Alberta is riding the biggest boom this country has ever known. I doubt whether the men and women who built the province could ever have imagined her present wealth and power, no matter how wild their dreams of the future or how tall their stories about the promise of this new land.

Those first pioneers, an unlikely but spirited group, celebrated Alberta's first day as a province on 1 September 1905 in the frantic fashion one would expect of a frontier. Along with twelve thousand other true believers in this "Last Best West" that they had first seen on posters back East, they toasted and sang to her health. They listened proudly as Sir Wilfrid Laurier paid his respects to this newest partner in the great Dominion of Canada, and then they proceeded hastily home to prepare for the inauguration ball that evening at Edmonton's Thistle Curling Rink. The ball had been touted as the biggest "do" that this part of the world was likely to see for some time. There had been a bit of a problem in organizing it—the closest florist was in Winnipeg, and a curling rink left on its own wasn't much for conjuring up visions of the great future that all the speakers had insisted the province could look forward to. But the women of the new capital city (which only a few years earlier had been a rather unseemly fur trade post) rose to the occasion. Muskrat, wolf, lynx, arctic fox—millions of dollars in pelts from the barons of the northern trade, the Revillon Frères and the Hudson's Bay Company—lined the curling rink walls in triumph. My grandparents, Gertrude and Balmer Watt, missed that first night. They arrived by winter to start the *Saturday News,* one of four Edmonton newspapers that they were to run in the turbulent first fifteen years of the province's life. The Watts didn't have much money, just a lot of enthusiasm and ambition, and in the early days of Alberta that went a long way.

In the staid Ontario they had left, the time had long since passed when a man of modest means could build a printing press and launch a competitive newspaper. Like most sectors of the economy, control of the media had been concentrated in the hands of the very rich. But out here on the western frontier, one could publish, edit, and do most of the writing for a paper. And people would read it—read it avidly. For one brief period my grandparents had two newspapers going at the same time, she the *Mirror*, he the *Saturday News*, both weeklies that fed on the energies of a multicultural readership as varied and unpredictable as the country itself. The pages were filled with the spectacle of an old world culture trying to transplant itself in a wilderness: the upwardly mobile urbanites of Edmonton banding together to build an opera house so that they could invite Sarah Bernhardt to perform in it; or desperate homesteaders watching their wagons and horses disappear into the quicksands of the mosquito-infested muskegs. They had all come west to find prosperity and the security they believed would come with it. They had come to build a new society.

As could be expected, there was immediate disagreement about what form that society should take. But a cold and hostile environment did wonders in convincing men to put differences aside. For a start, a nostalgia for people and places left far behind helped bring the new Albertans closer together. One needed some reassurance when one stepped out into the immense landscape. To their advantage was a boom-time atmosphere that made nearly anything seem possible, and there were no shortages of loan sharks to stake them in expanding whatever they had started. But one had to be careful. These economic adventures were dangerous, especially when tied to a staples economy. There was little manufacturing in the West, and Albertans were to learn the hard way that they had to diversify—they couldn't afford to put all their eggs in one basket.

The prairies were to be swept by many booms, but unfortunately these different forays into an uncertain international market place had one thing in common—instability and brevity. One could be rich one moment and poor the next. Demands for a product one had gambled everything on could disappear as quickly and mysteriously as they had appeared. And when the game radically changed, only a few were lucky or advantaged enough to be able to swim from one wave to the next. Most were left behind. And as the dreams faded, devastating droughts and terrible winters aged people quickly. In fact, most of the pioneers only had a single brief fling at their dream of independence. Distant politicians and captains of industry, absentee landlords, and speculators could bring everything down with an overnight shift in corporate policy. And when things turned bad, the banks and loan companies were quick to turn on you and foreclose. The West was still a colony of the East; the decisions that affected the course of her history were taken elsewhere. The independence of the frontier was an illusion.

In 1913 my grandparents lost their last paper. She opened a succession of small businesses, selling anything from antiques to canaries. He hired on as assistant editor of the *Edmonton Journal*, the Toronto-controlled paper in the Southam chain that he had felt so confident he could outrun. He was never to put out another newspaper of his own. He soon became the editor of the *Journal*, worked hard for thirty years (even helped win a Pulitzer Prize for the newspaper) but now it was for a succession of eastern publishers who were sent out to manage a revenue paper.

Like so many other Albertans of the time, he was left in a curious predicament. He had found the new country he had come looking for, and yet he hadn't. Alberta was still "tomorrow country"—but the tomorrow in question now seemed much more distant on the horizon. The province was heading into a series of boom/depression cycles that would culminate in the terrible years of the thirties. These pioneers were to have to witness the collapse of everything they had worked so hard to build.

By 1935 the land that had once promised everything seemed worthless—promotion brochures no longer outdid themselves to describe its future. But the people somehow held on. Earlier visions of wealth and prosperity changed to a simple sense of home, of friends, of belonging—a faith that things had to turn for the better. The land, at times so severe, nonetheless held them. Its rail lines and roads still stretched as far as the eye could see, somehow always promising something around the next bend. To many, the landscape "as open as day" was a relief from the closed and vicious economic system that held them in its grip. And in those enormous, almost empty spaces, a distinct culture was emerging—a culture born of a great deal of suffering, but with a stubborn streak and a spirit for survival. At the centre of this culture were the stories and tall tales people told each other, accounts in which reality got twisted beyond recognition yet in which the truth always could be found. For a time the future of the province lay in their exaggeration and good humour. The stories were repeated again and again, through the toughest times, always changing to suit the fancy of a new teller.

The characters of this book tell their versions of these stories. Rudy Wiebe works with what he knew or heard first as a boy and then as an award-winning writer living in a number of locations across the province. Yet he doesn't leave things as he found them. His stories come forward in time to speak to the present and future of the province as much as to its past. A farm wife, a premier, the child of a poor family, an explorer, a populist philosopher, an Indian chief, and a holiday camper—all describe their feelings about the place. The stories are at once fiction and fact, in the best tradition of what Alberta has always held out to its faithful.

Long after my grandfather had resigned himself to what had happened to his businesses, he used to speak of the tragedy of the unseeing eye, of the person who just didn't have the time or disposition to see things—who couldn't see his history for what it was and who often couldn't even enjoy the beauty of his surroundings. My grandfather never ceased to be captivated by this province. He travelled it extensively and never became tired of it. He was always very conscious of belonging here. The photographs of Harry Savage have that same sense of belonging, of being right for the place. They don't get carried away with all the glitter and bluster of the new Alberta. It's there, but in its place as only a part of the province's fascination. Savage has an eye for Alberta that comes from forty-one years of living here as a photographer and painter. His roots run deep, from the quiet, small-town Alberta of the forties and fifties to the booming, bustling cities of the sixties and seventies.

He captures a sense of detail and character truly accessible only to the native—his photographs a vision of a landscape transformed. Light moves across the prairie like a paintbrush, pinpointing a road, a fence line, a distant range of hills. Each landscape has a feeling all its own, often reflecting some aspect of the spirit of the people who lived on it—the Indians who paid homage to it, the farmers and town builders who first tried to subdue it, then later learned how to live with it.

Savage's photographs and Wiebe's stories are as much an elegy for the things we have lost in the first seventy-five years as they are a celebration of the Alberta we have won. But then, is it possible to have the one without the other? My grandfather retired in 1946, the year I was born, and spent many of the following years showing a young boy some of what he knew of life along the many trails that then wandered through the Saskatchewan River valley in downtown Edmonton. It was a time to reflect on fifty turbulent years—watching the ice go out on the river each spring, sitting in the evening on the old green "Rest and Read the Journal" benches that dotted the edge of the valley, listening to the cries of the great flocks of geese that flew over the city on their way north. For me, it was a time to learn from the stories that carried the pain and the accomplishment of those many years, to meet in this man's gentle and thoughtful manner the people who had settled the West.

This book presents the character of those people, the vast spaces and weather-beaten faces that have been our history. Its spirit is out there in the open country, where our ancestors—visionaries and ordinary men and women—came to try to improve upon the past, to create a new world, a new world they hoped would be measured by more than mere affluence and power. Some will say that they failed, but it is in their failures as much as in their successes that the romance of this beautiful province is to be found.

TOM RADFORD
Edmonton, 1979

Acknowledgement

As will be obvious to anyone with a casual knowledge of Alberta history, I did not invent many of the incidents in the stories included here; I simply discovered them and have retold them in my own way. Some of these discoveries were made while reading, others during the summers our family has spent camping about the province. I would like to acknowledge a particular debt to the following storytellers: G. Blake, J. Chancelet, H. Dempsey, G. Garcia-Marquez, R. Gard, E. and P. Holmgren, W. Gladstone, J. McDougall, J. Martin, F. Oliver, S. Roberts. To them, both living and dead, my sincere thanks.

There are innumerable stories to find and it is always impossible to tell them all. My son Christopher, who was on most of our travels, lived through one particular story which is not included here. Its title would have to be "The Midnight Gunman of the Hand Hills," but it, like many other stories about Alberta, still remains to be told.

RUDY WIEBE
Calgary, 1979

Looking south over the Canada–U.S. border to Big Chief
Mountain. Some of the most beautiful ranching and farming
country in the world is to be found in this area, which was
settled by Mormons who migrated from Utah in 1887.

Above: Evening falls on the Rockies west of Mountain View, a
tiny hamlet which was first registered in 1894.

Opposite: The wide-open spaces of the grassland prairie stretch
to the horizon south of Walsh, near the Saskatchewan border.

Aspen forest in Elk Island National Park, east of Edmonton.
One of the most wooded areas in central Alberta, the park is
noted for its beautiful lakes, a lovely nine-hole golf course, and
a large herd of buffalo.

Raspberries picked in the Glory Hills, west of Edmonton.

Upper: Folk dancers from many different backgrounds
perform throughout the province.

Lower: Old-timers enjoy a chat at the Innisfail Fair, one of the
many agricultural exhibitions that add flavour to an Alberta
summer.

Upper: Wearing a blouse embroidered in traditional Ukrainian style, a judge surveys the contestants during summer festivities.

Lower: The traditions of many countries are kept alive in this young province. In the heat of summer, young competitors perform Highland dances.

Steer wrestling always draws the crowds at the Hand Hills
Stampede. In terms of consecutive years, this is the oldest
stampede in Alberta.

A storm threatens at Spring Coulee, in the southwest corner of
the province. The community was so named because of the
numerous springs which bubbled up in the coulee running
through the settlement.

Cowpunchers drive cattle near the hamlet of Twin Butte on the edge of the foothills. This dirt road lies just off Highway 6, between Pincher Creek and Waterton Lakes, a highway which offers thirty of the loveliest miles of driving in the province.

Downtown Calgary, seen from the southwest. Now an
international metropolis, Calgary stands on the site where just
over a hundred years ago a detachment of the North-West
Mounted Police built a fort at the confluence of the
Bow and Elbow rivers.

Farms and ranches roll up to the foot of the Rockies south of Cowley.

Rain clouds gather over a lone granary near Milk River. The
great sweep of the surrounding countryside makes this one of
the most awe-inspiring parts of southern Alberta.

Grain elevators near Coutts, in the heart of the grassland
prairie. The community was named after Baroness
Burdett-Coutts, an English peeress who was a stockholder in
the Alberta Railway and Irrigation Company.

The Crees called this country *michichi ispatinan*—the Hand Hills—because the shape of the hills and coulees reminded them of the outstretched fingers of a hand.

Horses on the range, near Westward Ho.

Edmonton at dusk. The city's origins go back to the early
fur-trading days when the first Edmonton House was built in
1795 twenty miles downstream from the present site
of the provincial capital.

The Oil Capitals of Canada

The oil capitals of Canada are of course in Alberta, and they both tell you what they are on nice large billboards, it doesn't matter from what direction you drive in. The signs are lit up bright at night and that's really important around December when there are only seven or eight hours between sunrise and sunset anyway. Of course that's balanced by the more or less round-the-clock-twice daylight of June, but when you drive a car and the snow has been slashing out of the darkness at you for miles, it makes you feel nice and warm just to see those signs, "Welcome to Calgary, Oil Capital of Canada!". . ."Welcome to Edmonton, Oil Capital of Canada!" And since they're 297 kilometres apart, you're not likely to see them at the same time and wonder.

If you fly in, Calgary wins hands down. As the plane taxis to an airport that's so modern it's out of date already, you suddenly see three oil donkeys, close together, pumping relentlessly. No sign, no word, just those pumps so close to the ramp that a 747 has to time it just right or its wing-tip will get heavily nudged. Neither Edmonton Industrial nor International has anything so ominously stunning.

I almost never fly, but I know the roads of Alberta better than the stubble I scrape off my face every other morning. Since the fifties the roads here are probably the best in Canada and the gas is cheaper, by twenty cents, than anywhere else so I'm like the average Albertan in that way, around on wheels most of the time and most likely in a pick-up at that. I was born and have lived here all my life—away just long enough in 1943-45 to learn that the mud of Holland was something I never wanted to slog through again, especially while getting shot at— but don't ask me to explain Calgary and Edmonton. A lot of people living in them now moved in from far away, but still the largest number are like me: born on Alberta farms or in small towns and come to live in them for the jobs, the money, the good living. That one prairie province should have two such big places, so much alike and so different, is kind of amazing.

Edmonton got going first, 1790s, because the Hudson's Bay Company wanted to trade with the Indians but was too scared of the Blackfeet (there was a good reason: four different posts got burned down) so they stayed north among the friendly Crees on the North Saskatchewan. Calgary started in 1875 when the North-West Mounted Police built a little fort where the Elbow River runs into the Bow so that they could chase out the American traders killing the same Blackfeet with disease and rotgut whisky. Then in 1883 Calgary got the CPR transcontinental. Edmonton had to wait till 1891 to get the railroad—from Calgary!—but Edmonton got the government in 1905 and, by Premier Rutherford's sharp trick, the university two years later. Calgary always had the prairie and the foothills and then eastern money and ranching; Edmonton always had the deep black soil of the parkland and then the Ukrainians and mixed farming, but the big action, so Calgarians say, started southwest of Calgary in 1914 when the Dingman Well opened up the Turner Valley oil field. Edmontonians will tell you it started southwest of Edmonton in 1947 when Discovery No. 1 blew in the Leduc oil field. So now the two cities anchor either end of the four/six-lane highway that's the north/south stem of the province (or you can fly between them in thirty-five minutes either direction, every hour) and Calgary will tell you it's got all the oil company headquarters and Edmonton that it's got all the refineries. They're both right, of course; even.

My grandfather Blake came west after the Riel so-called Rebellion got everybody in Ontario excited about the North-West Territories and he was lucky: he met Dan Riley (later Senator) who gave him a job wintering cattle up the Highwood River and then my grandma saved him from the lonely and dissolute life of a cowpuncher. At least that's my grandma's version, and she outlived him by twenty-seven years so it mostly holds in the family. She was the fourth English governess the Cochrane Ranch brought into the country (the first three got married away too) but my grandfather always said she wrestled him down to a homestead and look at what happened: such a big spread on Mosquito Creek, the home place and the township of lease land running with chunky English Herefords and the log house they built so full of English books that he never had time, one year to the next, even to ride into Nanton for a drink. Nothing but work, work, and raise four sons to try and keep ahead of more work. I was William son of William, second son of second son, and after Holland I tried working on that family ranch. The Stoney Indians call the foothill country west of Nanton and High River "Paradise." They say there the Great Spirit made all the women and put them into one big ravine and then he made all the men and put them in another one and they lived like that, apart, until one day a woman met a man hunting. They told each other how lonely their camps were, and that night all the men moved to the women's ravine. I don't know why they didn't move the other way around but that, the Stoneys say, was The Beginning of Things.

I can believe it. I've never seen anything like standing on one of those hills, the white mountains shining behind you and the long green hills levelling out with creeks and rivers to the prairie as far away as you can see, the horizon misting away until it slips into sky, and the cattle all over the round hills grazing. I remember one fall roundup, when we trailed our herds down from the mountains the sun was rising, the scarlet edge of it just a paper cut on the golden horizon and the light spraying up like glory; it made you feel like doing what the Indians sometimes did: lie down on a high rock and die. But I couldn't work there; the place was too small for all the grandchildren and half my lungs and most of one leg was gone from the war. I had to try something in the city.

Calgary then was clumped down in the Bow/Elbow valleys, a few clusters of big houses on Mount Royal and all the little places no farther west than the Louise Bridge with the CPR Palliser Hotel the tallest building downtown, like it had been for forty years, and the Grain Exchange kitty-corner from it second. "Sandstone City" they called it before World War I, and the best business fronts along 8th and 9th Avenue were still that; nothing much had happened since the fast cheap building boom of the twenties, and Leduc with all the new eastern and American money hadn't started to move much yet. There were lots of ads in the *Herald* and the *Albertan* for "seismic crews," and I had no idea what that meant but went around anyway and they took one look at my leg and said sorry. A couple of the exploration men, veterans too, tried to give me desk jobs and I finally took one, a kind of woman's job (I thought then) talking on the radio-telephone and trying to keep track of where everything and everybody was with all the new expensive equipment, but after a few months I couldn't take it. Everything was running crazy, everything should have been done an hour ago if not yesterday, there was paper falling off my table and piling up in the corners of the closet where I couldn't move my chair, just swivel around in and out, and they were always making new strikes that made anything they'd found till then look like peanuts—as if the whole earth under Alberta was one hellish fire and if they only poked a pipe down deep enough it would explode out, flaming gas and oil on everybody. After a while when the telephone rang such a strange grimace would come over my boss's face that finally I realized what it was: greed.

There's a world in every city, rich Alberta too, that fits in/around/between the obvious one of everyday business, of the ordinary people who make up the solid core of any working world and pay their taxes and have some civic pride and make sure the buildings are warm and maintained. It's a world these ordinary people—you—walk past/through a dozen times a day and you'll never notice it because maybe you don't want to and anyway it tries, with all the skill it has left, to fit between the spaces your world leaves so it won't get noticed. But it's there all the time downtown, and sometimes in the evening and at night when it really comes out you can't help seeing it. It's the world of the derelict, the "bum" as most people call it but that name doesn't mean as much as the other, a world mostly of men because women usually don't let themselves go in that way and if they do they do what they have to in small closed rooms they pay for by the hour so you hardly see them unless you go looking for them; the world of scavenging, of rescue missions, of cheap wine and rubbing alcohol.

I had a bit of veteran's pension, like many of the men I met—you sometimes have a partner for a while in that world but you never live with anyone—but toward the end of the month I'd be stealing after-shave lotion from the night drugstores and sometimes in winter I got thirty warm days in the crowbar hotel out of that, but terrible days too because then you're forced cold turkey dry. After a while the taller buildings of Calgary's boom that's still going on started to pile up, all around us, between the abandoned businesses and houses where we lived in the summers to save the two bits a Salvation Army bed would cost, but the only difference to us was that the construction workers sometimes gave us a dime. They're usually easier to touch than the up-and-running businessmen because they usually walk down the street in bunches, bragging to each other and they won't look at you to admit you're there, but if you ever get one of them alone you—

Two weeks ago I was in Edmonton at the Chateau Lacombe and after breakfast, before the meeting I was there for, all of a sudden I got this terrible longing to walk along the top of the river bank again, the places I can never forget anyway. It's all changed now of course. Where the old public library and the Edmonton Club once stood is the AGT tower, thirty-seven stories up, but the brush below the Macdonald Hotel was still there, bare brown with autumn but still thick enough to hide you and sure enough the path was still worn and I came around the cement corner of the air vent below the Mac—and there is a man, I knew it, squatting against the grating like we used to, and not too badly dressed because these heavy nylon parkas now wear well and keep their colour even when they're slick with dirt. He is gnawing a small bone carefully, chicken I think, a tall can of hairspray on the ground beside him. Nine-thirty in the morning, the cloudless autumn sun hitting him straight on warm and the blast of air from the vent so moist and hot my glasses fog, again and again. At least I think it's from the air. He glances up and his eyes change, as I know mine always did when I saw a comfortable Canadian man facing me alone, but he has a nice little routine. He drops the bone between his boots and digs in his parka pocket, studies the three coins he finds there, then looks up smiling pathetically. Under the bulgy parka, inside his big solid skull he looks terribly sick.

"I got twenty-seven cents for starters," he says. "If I had two bits more . . . ."

I have to say something; I can only gesture at the hairspray.

"Why'd you . . . get that?"

"Last night. I don't feel so good now," he says. "I kinda lost my head there, last night."

"You've got to eat food, solid food," I say and he sees the five-dollar bill in my hand. His tone changes:

"My god man, I'll pray for you every day, I'll get some real good food, I know just the place that'll—"

"Don't promise!" I'm yelling at him now. I have to get out of here. "Just get some food!"

It was stupid of me to walk along here, what got hold of me? I get up the path and onto Jasper Avenue screaming traffic and across it by a dug-out space where they're putting together the steel crane to build a skyscraper and past that there's the new Citadel Theatre, all square glass and open for everyone in the world to see how beautiful everything here is. I get behind some hoarding so I can cry in peace.

Well, I never said I was an Alberta he-man with gravel and concrete in my jaw. Or head. Actually, most people you'll meet out here aren't either. I grew up in the foothills, parents, uncles, aunts, cousins, family all around and not one of the so-called Big Four ranchers in the bunch. I never knew what hunger was, or want, and my grandma telling me stories about cowboys and dukes and Indians and a Prince of Wales and storekeepers like they had always belonged together, just naturally. But I lost myself; something went wrong in the world I saw growing around me and I lost myself, I didn't really understand how or care maybe till very early one morning, autumn like this, when I noticed a bent old man leaning over one of those garbage cans they bolt onto lampposts, digging down carefully and I looked and looked and all of a sudden I knew I was looking through plate glass at myself. I *saw my self*, if you get what I mean. When I got myself back home then my mother couldn't say anything, just "Billy . . . Billy . . ." and my father came into the room and looked at me in the bed and after a while he said, "We all thought years ago you were dead."

In my grandma's library that winter I discovered my namesake:

William Blake, the English poet.

> Does the Eagle know what is in the pit?
> Or wilt thou go ask the Mole?
> Can Wisdom be put in a silver rod?
> Or Love in a golden bowl?

and

> He who binds to himself a joy
> Does the winged life destroy;
> But he who kisses the joy as it flies
> Lives in eternity's sun rise.

and my favourite, I think:

> I laid me down upon a bank
> Where love lay sleeping.
> I heard among the rushes dank
> Weeping, Weeping.
>
> Then I went to the heath and the wild,
> To the thistles and thorns of the waste
> And they told me how they were beguil'd,
> Driven out, and compel'd to be chaste.

So the fall after that I was at the University of Alberta, a bit long in the tooth but not too much out of the veteran line. Some English architect, I believe, was once hired to plan a kind of imitation Oxford Colonial on the south bank of the North Saskatchewan and they actually built a few buildings at opposite sides of a possible quadrangle before the poplars and the river valley got too much for them and they scattered buildings around odd clearings. When I got there it was mostly quonset huts between the distant brick, but there were good songs in Mixed Chorus for the bass voice I found I had and several professors knew Blake enough not to ruin him. I became a teacher, high school by mistake for two years and then grade five ever after.

Twenty years, watching the city sprout up higher than the Legislative Building out of the oil-soaked ground in glass and concrete all along "the beautiful river valley that makes Edmonton," as Bob Kroetsch writes so carefully, "one of the three most beautiful cities in Canada. It is a valley that on a January morning might shelter ten thousand buffalo. Edmonton with its high towers illumined at six o'clock on a winter's night is a blue-green vision of a city, hung from the stars above a black chasm." I couldn't say it any better so I won't try. Twenty years, and then I said to my wife, "Let's take a year off."

"What?" she said, quite loud for her.

"Wouldn't it be nice, a year in Calgary?"

"Well. . . ." She was born in Edmonton.

We rented out the bungalow we had bought long ago for twice the old mortgage payments (rent in Edmonton is unbelievable now) and for the extra we leased a very small house under the Bow valley bluffs, Sunnyside, across the river from downtown. I sold our truck camper for $4,800 and that means we've got $400 a month to live on, plus about $50 extra from savings. I hope the Ford doesn't break down, we need it to visit all the cousins in Nanton (they always say, "Go ahead, fill up at the yard tank," and I do, I gladly accept gifts) and to take young Bill to hockey practices and games. His coach doesn't wear a white Stetson, at least not behind the players' bench, but he's a genuine Calgarian of a certain kind.

"That kid of yours, he's so terrific, big, strong, if he'd just push himself a little he'd be the second coming of Bobby—"

"He doesn't want to be terrific," I try to comfort him.

"Did you see that shift, did you see, he shifted that winger right out of his jockstrap, did you. . . ."

Thank god young Bill has more sense. If he really put his back into it somebody would show up with half a million dollars and wreck him for good. Out of our living-room window through the trees on Prince's Island we can see all the squarish skyscrapers. Some smart alec in a big eastern paper (not the silly one that tried to count all the bathroom taps made of gold that were sold here), this guy wrote that

Calgary would be a city all right as soon as they got around to uncrating it; but if you walk north up Nose Hill you get the right view of things. Don't drive; walk through the prairie grass in autumn or in the first light snow of November and feel your muscles work inside your jeans against the cold so you've got hard proof you're alive. Up there you'll see that even if another seventy office skyscrapers get knocked up, as they say they will, even if one of them is half again as high as the Calgary Tower and there's a million people spread out of the valley and onto the flats, most of them at least will stop trying to crawl to work in single cars all at the same time: they're planning Light Rail Transit now just like Edmonton already is building, and no matter what happens the hills can't be destroyed, nor the hundred miles of mountains you can see stretched down the west and totally unbothered by people. No world is really changed by money and skyscrapers: not if you don't want it to be.

The oil capitals of Canada. I have to laugh. They're right, of course, both of them, and soon they'll be grown up enough to know they don't have to mention it. I used to get so mad at people knocking Alberta, and a few years ago when the Ford was new I drove one of those bigwig speakers we always get to our teachers' conventions back to his hotel in Edmonton. It was February, a nice solid cold front well settled in and he'd been in Calgary the day before offering freely for a big fee of all his wisdom there. The wind was coming straight as a knife down the valley from the Arctic, the tires groaned and bumped on the High Level Bridge like they do in a windchill of about seventy below. He just hunched up there, curled inside his coat in the warm car. Finally he delivered himself:

"Why the hell'd anybody ever try to build cities up here?"

I just had to laugh in his face. It isn't polite but I figured somebody owed him that, it might as well be me that paid.

"You'll never know," I told him. "Not if you haven't the guts to live here."

Lake Isle of Innisfree

The Canadian Northern Railway built through Del Norte the summer of 1905 and it came right through my homestead on the east-west road under the hill where travellers had been stopping for the six, seven years we'd been trying to make a living there. Actually, my wife ran the Del Norte post office out of our house and that plus wagons stopping overnight helped us make it. But then they wanted to move the post office to the tracks of course, and we thought maybe we could get a town started. Elevators, stores, everything, and the Canadian Northern said sure so all us farmers were happy. But Mannville and Vermilion were down the line east and Vegreville west so Del Norte couldn't seem to get going. The trains roared through and we hardly even had any wagons stopping by for three, four years. Then one spring day a train with a private car stopped and Sir Byron Edmund Walker and ten, twelve reporters got off.

He wasn't actually "Sir" at the time; King Edward VII knighted him a year later but he was already so important I've always thought of him as—well, at sixty he was president of the Canadian Bank of Commerce plus president of the Canadian Bankers Association and vice-president of the American Bankers Association, and also chairman of the Board of Governors of the University of Toronto and of the Trustees of the National Art Gallery and one of the founders of the Royal Ontario Museum—a list of everything he was doing, and did after, would fill a book but they say he is the main reason Canada has seven, eight big banks with branches everywhere and not the thousands of small local banks they have in the States where hundreds regularly go broke and you lose everything.

Anyway, when Sir Edmund stopped his private car at Del Norte he was looking for towns where he could build branches of the Bank of Commerce. He said to me he wanted to see the town so I said come on up the hill. Most of those reporters started with us but by the time we got to the top on that rough path there was only him and me left.

The hill's all covered with poplars now. When we first moved there it was bare as any prairie but by 1908 they were already shoulder-high, and as far as you could see from the top there were more and more trees growing, everywhere. The farmers' fields were black-and-tan patches and the trees shimmering yellowish green because there weren't any fires any more, and long, long no buffalo, to keep those tough poplars from spreading. The lakes lay blue in hollows, the land all around us rolling beautiful like the green knuckled back of God's hand my wife used to say. I told Sir Edmund that.

He was looking as if he wanted to remember forever. Then he pointed to Birch Lake a mile or two away. Its little islands had always had a bristle of trees on them even when all the rest was bare prairie.

"That looks just like my summer place," he said. "In Ireland. Innisfree, beauty . . . beauty . . . ."

He was so quiet, I looked at him. In size he wasn't even as big as me: soft grey suit and that climb had hardly put a speck of dirt on his shining shoes. He seemed to be looking past the horizon; the way some people can when the land doesn't scare them.

> "I will arise and go now, and go to Innisfree,
> And a small cabin build there, of clay and wattles made:
> Nine bean-rows will I have there, a hive for the honeybee,
> And live alone in the bee-loud glade.
>
> And I shall have peace there, for . . . ."

I hadn't heard of William Yeats then but I know poetry when I hear it, and he just stopped saying it for some reason. Below us were the ten, twelve buildings of the town and the red elevator with "DEL NORTE" on it and the tracks straight till out of sight in either direction. Just an ordinary day in Alberta, clear as rubbed glass.

"Mr. Puckette," he said suddenly. "I was my father's oldest son, born on a farm in Seneca County, Ontario, and I left school at twelve to work for my uncle and . . . ."

I was going to tell him I never got past grade five either but I could see what he had started was far too personal for a big man like him to blurt out to a stranger on a prairie hill, no matter how beautiful. So I shut up and let him say what he suddenly wanted to tell me.

"Mr. Puckette," and he was looking me straight in the eye then, "you tell your community that if you rename this town 'Innisfree,' I'll build you the most beautiful bank on the prairie."

Well, I got him to write that name for I sure didn't know how to spell it and then we shook hands and walked down. You should have heard those farmers holler when I told them. You'd have thought "Del Norte" fell on us from heaven instead of something somebody already dead had remembered from Colorado. Nobody even knew what it meant till I wrote to the new university in Edmonton and a month later found out it was really the tail end of Spanish "Rio Grande del Norte": Great River of the North. What could that mean to us? The North Saskatchewan was big enough but thirty miles away and there wasn't a Spaniard around, anywhere. There's no Irish either somebody yelled, which was true. Were we going to let some eastern bigshot tell us what to call our place when it'd had a perfectly good name for at least ten years?

"You better call it Innisfree," my wife said knitting our kids the usual winter socks. "You'll never see that Mr. Walker again anyway, and you just might get a bank out of it."

She was right, on both counts. Sir Edmund's word was as solid as his bank. Come and see it. Standing over seventy years, the hill high and green behind it. And still the most beautiful town bank on the prairies.

They Just Won't Believe

I don't know why but Albertans are known as being big liars. Maybe lately there is some reason for it, writers like Bill Mitchell and Bob Kroetsch telling stories here now, but there was a lot of liar talk going around already over a hundred years ago, like for example the two sons of the Reverend George McDougall. He was the Methodist missionary that froze to death in a buffalo hunt by Nose Creek in 1876. His sons were called the three biggest liars on the Canadian prairie, son David being one and son John the other two. Well, David was a businessman, so okay you can believe that, but John was an ordained minister, for two years chairman of the Canadian Methodist Assembly. I mean, really.

Actually, I think a lot of this liar business comes from Alberta nature. People who've never lived here can't believe the most natural stuff that happens, like big mosquitoes. There was a carpenter from Ontario name of August Bessai come to work on the heavy oil pilot plant at Cold Lake. One day he finally got tired of knocking mosquitoes aside with two-by-fours and crawled into an oil barrel to get some rest. When the brutes drilled their stingers through the barrel at him, he just bent them over with his hammer and for a while he was okay. But he only did that to seven mosquitoes, and then they flew away with the barrel. Any Albertan would have taken his hacksaw in there, but easterners, they just don't believe.

Or a perfectly natural thing like the power of the Alberta sun. Dick Harrison, a Peace River farmer, made a rawhide harness for his team and he was halfway up the Dunvegan Hill with a load of wheat when a cloud came up and it started to rain. Of course, that wet rawhide started to stretch. He finally got the horses to the top, but it was a real soaker and those rawhide traces had stretched so much his heavy wagon had slid back all the way to the bottom of the hill, a mile and a half down. The rain stopped just then, so he knew he had to work fast. He got the harness off the horses and buckled it onto a big spruce just as the sun came out and he barely had time to roll and smoke a cigarette before the heat of the sun had shrunk that rawhide right up and brought that load up Dunvegan Hill so fast he had to cut the traces or the wagon would have smashed into the spruce.

People outside Alberta won't believe that. They've heard stories about our chinooks for over a hundred years and you'd think—David McDougall in 1877 told them how that winter he drove a sleigh and team from Morley to Fort Calgary and the chinook blew down through the Kicking Horse Pass and started licking up the snow so fast he whipped those horses to a dead run and they could barely stay ahead of it. His horses were ploughing snow, the front runners of his sleigh were floating easy on a river of water, and the back runners were dragging up such a dust that his dog running behind choked to death in the dust storm. Eighteen seventy-seven, and other Canadians are calling that a lie to this day! They could come out here any winter, but oh no...it's like our premier said just the other day, they just won't believe *nothing* about Alberta till they see it on the TV.

Well, if nobody believes stories about our nature, they believe even less about our people. Like Eric Harvie, for instance. This silly story has been around for about forty years that Eric Harvie became our biggest oil millionaire by a legal accident: that instead of being paid lawyer's fees of something like forty-eight thousand dollars, he took over the mineral rights to some Alberta land from an English company—absentee capitalists, of course—and then they found both the Leduc *and* Redwater oil fields under it. Harvie had those mineral rights, okay, but do you actually believe a lawyer raised an Ontario Methodist would skip that kind of fee by accident, in 1943 dollars? You have to be crazy.

I'll tell you what really happened, and if you've had a hard time with what I've told you so far, I don't know what you'll do with this. Eric Harvie was born in 1892, in Ontario. That wasn't his fault, of course, and he left Orillia for the West as soon as he was old enough and graduated from law at the University of Alberta in 1914. He was wounded in the elbow, knee, and hip in the Battle of the Somme (1916) and had a fever all his life, about once a year, from that. He was so careful as a lawyer he wouldn't even smile during business hours, it might give a client the wrong idea, but with his own money he was a gambler. Not the idiotic, lottery, slot-machine kind: he gambled on the resources of this province, especially oil, right from the start. So in 1921 he was in with R.B. Bennett—later prime minister of Canada—and the Turner Valley oil field, in 1925 with Home Oil at Wainwright, 1928 at Lloydminster, and Vermilion in 1941. All these fields were small, but Harvie put his legal head and money into every one of them and in 1943 he took the gamble that could have wrecked him as easy as it made him the richest man in Alberta, some say Canada.

The Social Credit government about 1941 set a tax on mineral rights of half a cent per acre. That doesn't sound like much, but this English outfit called the Western Land Company owned rights to 487,342.8 acres. By 1943 they were going to let those rights revert to the government for taxes when Harvie heard about it and offered them ten thousand dollars; they sold immediately, but then Harvie was stuck with all the back and ongoing taxes. He paid over a hundred thousand on his "Moose Pasture," as he called it, to keep the titles clear before he finally persuaded Imperial to drill, and on February 13, 1947, Discovery No. 1 exploded at Leduc. That's no accident, that's high-roller gambling. They drilled 1,278 wells at Leduc-Woodbend, most of them on Harvie's rights, and when Redwater blew in, four times the size of Leduc and dead centre on Harvie rights that Shell Oil had once tested and told him were completely useless—reporters suddenly started figuring Harvie was worth about fifty million dollars, take or give ten. By 1954, from rights sales, organizing so many companies nobody except he could keep track of them, and a steady flow of oil royalties, they figured he was over a hundred million dollars. And that's when the strangest thing of all happened.

He started giving the money away. He always kept his hand in—

organized Western Minerals to drill the first holes north of the Arctic Circle, for example—but he started big giving through foundations he organized: the Glenbow to collect paintings, artifacts, manuscripts, photographs—anything of western history value—and the Devonian doing things like underwriting cold-ocean research in Newfoundland, building a Fathers of Confederation Centre in Charlottetown and a glassed-in park in downtown Calgary; he set up statues to Robert the Bruce and General James Wolfe; through the Woods Foundation he donated both River and Heritage Park to Calgary—in fact, he gave so many millions away that in August 1974, *Time* magazine (you should believe it, it's American) called him "The-Man-Who-Gave-Everything-Back-And-Then-Some."

I'm not saying Harvie's family was—is—poor. No way, but after Leduc he and his wife never changed houses; he drove one car until it wore out and then he got another one. He hated publicity, honestly, and besides the hundred odd millions everybody knows he gave away there's probably as much again nobody knows about because he wouldn't talk. I watched him over thirty years, though we never said a word to each other, and I figure Eric Harvie was setting a new world style in millionaires. I mean, can you imagine J. Paul Getty or H.L. Hunt or Howard Hughes stopping piling it up so they could give it away? Well, nobody much in Alberta's followed him either, at least not yet. And when the press kept asking him, all he'd say was the province had been very good to him, why shouldn't he give it back?

I know this is harder to believe than any chinook story. Just don't bother Mrs. Harvie trying to check it out, she still lives in that house in Elbow Park, Calgary, or their children Donald, Neil, Joy. They're like Harvie, they don't talk to snoops, but you'll never see them in *the* places in London and New York either. And don't bother the Herron brothers who were in with him on the Turner Valley excitement in the twenties, or Jim Gray who tried twenty-five years for one good interview, or Jack Brooks who kept Harvie's bird dogs in his kennels for forty years, or—heck, three thousand people worked for Harvie at any given time, I can't name them all. If you're really interested, why don't you just go to the Glenbow Archives, 9th Avenue S.E., Calgary. It was built for twelve million dollars to store some (it's not big enough for all) of the things Harvie had collected, and he gave five million to keep it open for the public. The archivist there, Hugh Dempsey, tells me they're trying to persuade Mrs. Harvie to let them make a video-tape of Harvie's life, so you can watch it all in black and white.

That's the best proof I can give you, now. But I know that the good that people do lives after them, and I'm sure it'll be at least another three, four generations before the Harvie heirs change so much they become "personalities" and start fighting in public and stuff like that. So it'll be a while before the Toronto CBC will hear about him and make a TV documentary drama of his life so you can know for sure.

A farmer combines barley near Falher. Because of its short growing season, barley is a staple crop in northern Alberta.

A fog bank gathers above the town of Peace River. The river
flows through a beautiful countryside which became one of the
last homesteading frontiers of the West. To this day, the Peace
River country is associated with the "Last Best West."

The Canadian Pacific rail line at Manyberries in the
southeastern corner of the province.

Opposite: A horse-drawn binder at Fort Edmonton Historical Park epitomizes the strange phenomenon of a province that is only seventy-five years old yet whose history has to be sought out mainly in museums and amusement parks.

Above: The south shore of Lesser Slave Lake is the setting for the story "A History of the New World." It is in this region that Jean Labarge, the homespun philosopher, is sited as living.

Above: Long shadows foretell the approach of winter near
Hairy Hill. According to local histories, it was in these hills
that the buffalo used to shed their hairy winter coats
each spring.

Opposite: The town of Dorothy lies at the foot of the badlands
on the banks of the Red Deer River. The community was
named after the first girl born in the district.

Above: The post office at Buffalo, a lost community on the edge of the Suffield Military Experimental Range, a vast tract of unbroken prairie very similar to what the first settlers in the province must have encountered.

Opposite: This 75-year-old elm tree in the hamlet of Patricia is one of the first that was planted in the district.

Opposite: The Frank Slide, near Blairmore, gets its first dusting of snow three-quarters of a century after the face of Turtle Mountain fell on the mining town of Frank, killing eighty men, women, and children. Mining tragedies, especially the horror of the Hillcrest disaster, are the subject of the story "The Darkness Inside the Mountain."

Above: Infant mortality was common in isolated mining communities located far from the nearest doctor. This graveyard is at Mountain Park, now a ghost town.

Upper: Swathed wheat in the rich tabletop farmlands south of Drumheller.

Lower: Whistler swans take off after feeding, near Pine Lake.

Upper: Fallen leaves touched by the first frost.

Lower: The Pool elevator at Bluesky bears witness to the optimism of the men and women who named Alberta's small communities. The names Paradise Valley, Garden Plains, Sunnynook, Champion, and Valhalla are but a few of their creations.

The alkali sloughs south of Rentham are stopping places for
the great flocks of ducks and geese that migrate through the
province each spring and fall.

The farmer's goose is part of a wide variety of stock and
produce which are put on display each year at the
Millarville Fair.

Ice forms on the North Saskatchewan River at Shandro Bridge.

Chinook Christmas

The winter I turned nine was our first in southern Alberta, and the white scars of irrigation ditches circling lower and lower into the long, shallow hollow of our town uneven across the Canadian Pacific Railway seemed to me then like the trenches of some besieging army: the grey wrinkled snow driven there off the tilted fields, long, long welts carved in parallels below the square top of Big Chief Mountain sixty miles west where the implacable General of the Winds stood forever roaring at his troops: Advance! Relentless wind whining, roaring in one's head all fall, the trees bent so low east that one day I straightened up on the pedals of my bicycle and discovered I could stand motionless, balanced, the wind's weight a wall, a power that held me shivering uneasily facing into it.

But then I was nudged, pushed, clubbed and I let the wind wheel me round like always and I spread my arms akimbo, my jacket held wide at the waist and went no hands sailing along the gravel street, through three ridged stop corners on the fly to Jakie's house and leaned into his yard like a racing sloop, all canvas spread, and met him wobbling forward on his bike beside the little irrigation ditch that was filling their cistern for winter so I knocked him into that grey water and then he knocked me into it too.

"Let's ride to the main ditch," he said, trying to blink through the mud in his eyes.

"Sure," I said. "We'll get it anyways, we might as well get it good."

He was three years older than I and that summer we had become uneasy friends with the town's whole length of one-way wind between us because we were second cousins (twice removed at that, my father said, but for Canadian Mennonites that means a lot sometimes) and because of Anni and mostly because neither of us had any other friends. My sister Anni always knew what she wanted.

"We have to have a Christmas tree," she said. "How'll we ever find one here, nothing but sugarbeet fields and ditches?"

She was fourteen and the spring before when we left our bush homestead up north so my father could work on an irrigation dairy and Mama and Anni and I could thin beets, she had already been kissed there once or twice under a full moon, and she still thought that a good deal better than getting sunburned between endless beet rows, wrinkling up, hunched over like every other poor woman and child she saw stoop-shouldered in every field. Up north she and I always ploughed our Christmas tree out of the muskeg, our dog bounding high through soft cushions of snow, the air so motionless between the muskeg spruce—flounced, layered and blazing white with brown and green edges.

"There's a tree on old Heidebrecht's lawn," I said. "It's real pretty."

"Oh sure," and Anni sang, "Chop chop, hoora-a-a-il, Christmas in ja-a-a-il, how can we fa-a-a-il, they will throw out our heads in a pa-a-a-il."

"Anyways," I told her, "a Christmas tree isn't even Christian, it's heathen." Old Ema Racht—"Always Right" (but in Low German it rhymes: Ema Racht, Heidebrecht)—had the biggest Mennonite house in town; he had finally sold his farm to one of his sons for an unbeliev-able price—that was what he was mostly right at, buying low and sell-ing very high—and now he drove a black Buick to church twice every Sunday with his ancient daughter as stiff and erect as himself beside him; he always roared the motor until a cloud of bluish smoke was visible through the rear window before he slowly let out the clutch and began to move, shoving in the clutch a little as soon as the car threatened to go too quickly but never taking his foot off the gas. All summer his lawn, shaded by giant cottonwoods and blue-coned spruce, was bright green like a frog's belly.

"A Christmas tree's heathen? Who said, smarty head?" Anni twirled around me.

"In Sunday school, Mr. Rempel," I said. He was tall with broad shoulders and had "adorable," Anni had once confessed, curly blond hair.

That stopped her; for two seconds. But I saw immediately it was astonishment at my still holding that outdated opinion that was spreading like a cat's tongue licking over her face. She laughed aloud. "He's no fun," she said irrelevantly. "In fact, he's kinda dumb."

"How do you know?" I hit her with all I had: "You've never even *talked* to him."

"He's a curly blond," over her shoulder, going into the kitchen. I never had enough for Anni, of anything.

The Christmas kitchen was a whole pasture of smells gone crazy in spring, not only from two kinds of cookies, oatmeal with one chocolate chip topping each and pale almost brownly-bluish shapes of ammonia creatures Mama had let me stamp out of thick dough, but also cinnamon rolls with their bottoms up exuding sweet brown syrup and dimpled raisins like twirled targets to aim an uncontrollable finger at—"Mama, Eric's poking the rolls!"—and tiny square pyrushkis with their tops folded up into peaked and quartered little tents of ridged golden crust that oozed juices, red strawberry and royal purple saskatoon and pale creamy apple, how for the love of Christmas and stomach could anyone keep their hands—"Eric!"

And outside was chinook. The night before, a small bow of light had grown along the western horizon under the ceiling of clouds hammered down overhead like solid rafters; at the end of the day, the monolith of Big Chief Mountain sat for a moment against blue and an orange streak like a knife-tip about to slit open the rest of the horizon, a faint smell of crushed irrigated clover in summer slipping through to wander over the glazed drifts. And also a touch of warmth, very nearly a flare of mad possibility in the cold; today it blazed into actuality, my head huge as if its plates were unhinged for I could breathe that clover without sniffing after it, all the air burned with it, the drifts already wrinkling down into sodden sponges and the air swimming limpid like creek water on a May morning. Chinook! It fondled my bare head. Our chickens sang behind their windows, I opened the door and their acrid avian mist was swallowed whole, disappeared into the morning brilliance of chinook; our white-faced cow lifted her head above the dry alfalfa of her manger, her ears gesturing gently as they did whenever she was moved to ponderous liquid-eyed bovine contentment. Go on Boss, you bulgy hay-chewer, your warm flanks to butt my head against, your long soft teats swishing hot milk between my rhythmic fingers, go on you globed warm femaleness, and breathe all that spring, that momentary maddening spring the day before Christmas.

"There are still some trees left, Mrs. Orleski on her lot," I said to Anni, shifting the basket of *zweibach* to my other arm. She carried two pails of layered pastry for Tante Tien and though they were heavier, they were actually easier to carry because she could walk balanced. The basket in the basket of my bike would have been best, but the chinook had only licked the gravel street dry in blotches and left the rest wet, running everywhere under the snow-levelled ditches. It was everywhere slurp and slide and temptation to not catch your balance before you tucked your head and rolled soft and squitchy and were all over coated with three-times gumbo like your laden boots.

"She told us, a tree costs at least a dollar," Anni said.

"Yeah, the miserblist one, we'd never—"

"That's no word, 'miserblist.'"

"Miser-erbilist?"

"Miser-erb*a*list, rhymes with 'herb-*a*list,'" Anni sang, skipping a puddle too nonchalantly perhaps and slipping beautifully but sliding herself into balance so that nothing but her left pailbottom came up small gravel and heavy, heavy gumbo. We wiped it off with snow, left the food in Tante Tien's barren kitchen with her small horde of children rolling their small barbarian eyes at the steamy warmth of things and ran out before the small barbarian fingers could—"Eric and I have to get back because Mama needs us and Father is coming home right after supper and the. . . ." Anni had hauled me out with her long arm and swinging muddy pail and there was Jakie leaning against the cottonwood in the front yard, looking absolutely Chicago gangster to the very bend of his leg and cap pulled tight over his eyes.

"If you want a tree so bad," he said, "why don't you take it?"

Anni actually stopped and looked at him. Chinooks touch everyone differently: all he needed was a short machine gun.

"There's never nobody there at night," he said.

It was very hard to read Anni's expression, and Jakie must have made the same mistake I made because he continued, still looking at his fingernails which were very long and smooth with nice moons at their base, "Anyways, who'd miss one shitty little tree?"

"I presume," Anni said, and her tone warned me instantly, "I presume that if there is *never nobody* there, there must *always* be *somebody*, and I presume further that not even an habitual criminal would be so idiotic as to steal under such conditions, leave alone someone honest at Christmas when a chinook is blowing."

Her statement would have been stronger without either Christmas or chinook, and I think Anni felt so too because we hadn't left Jakie more than half a block behind, still leaning against the tree and studying the perfect moons of his fingernails, when she inexplicably commented, "He won't even get as far as his stupid dad, he'll just end up in jail."

"What's the matter with Oncle Willm?" I asked. To tell the truth, I liked Oncle Willm. He was certainly the strongest man in town, not much taller than me but so broad he walked sideways through any door and he could place his thick arms under half a beef and hoist it around and up onto a hook in one immense motion without breathing hard or slipping on the sawdust under his butcher's chopping block. Unlike any other Mennonite grown-up, he cracked jokes with me and so did Mrs. Cartwright who sold the meat for him. Mrs. Cartwright was always dressed so perfectly, her face as careful as a picture, and when she leaned over the counter, laughing, I always wanted to laugh with her like every man who bought meat there though I never saw a woman who did, her lips and teeth so red and white and marvellously, smoothly exact. She laughed like no woman I had ever seen, deeply, powerfully, her entire vivid body pushing itself out at me and moving with it until I felt tight and awkward, somehow—inexplicably then—ashamed.

"He's *not* our uncle thank Jehoshaphat," Anni snapped, and then seeing me goggle-eyed said quickly, "There's Mr. Ireland, let's catch a ride!"

Mr. Ireland's dray with its unmatched greys was moving toward the train station but it seemed that in any case Anni had intended not to go directly home but rather "downtown" as we called it—our town had three parallel streets south of the tracks and three north with avenues at right angles numbered 100 at the centre, and higher and lower on either side in anticipation of eventual more or less measure-less and endless expansion—so we hopped aboard and bounced along dangling our legs off the tailgate. The horses trotted while Mr. Ireland sang, the biggest grey plopping out hot steamy buns, and Mr. Ireland interrupted himself to mutter, "Enough time for that, Jock, get on with you!", slapping the mountainous rear gently with a flat rein, and they appeared behind the wagon under us in perfect single-file pattern like a queue of smooth-headed children, steaming slightly as they sank out of sight in the gumbo. The chinook blustered violently through trees and over a roof and suddenly Mr. Ireland roared with it as we passed the Japanese Buddhist church that was swallowing a snake of small brown children,

> "Oh, he shot her through the window,
> And the bullet's in her yet!"

and the dray sighed silently across Main Street at 101 Avenue on its fat balloon tires salvaged from World War II fighter planes. A huge black truck with its grain box standing tight full of Hutterites, beards and polka-dotted kerchiefs facing into the wind, rolled past and squitched all of a grey pothole at us, but missed.

"Do men have yets too?" I asked Anni.

"Yets?"

"He sang, 'the bullet's in her yet.'"

Anni laughed. "No," she spluttered, "only women. And you have to shoot them through their windows to hit their yets!"

But then, still laughing, she knocked one of our pails off and we had to jump anyways because we were passing the high front of the largest grocery and hardware store, Doerksen Bros. Props., and that's where Mrs. Orleski had her Christmas trees leaning against the wall. Mrs. Orleski usually sold Lethbridge *Heralds* at the corner for a nickel, perhaps two or three a day since Hermie Kudreck had the town sewed up with home delivery—Hermie owned a CCM three-speed by the time he was ten, a Harley-Davidson at fifteen, and an Olds convertible at nineteen, all starting from *Herald* saturation of our town—but when Doerksen Brothers started playing Christmas carols on the gramophone at the back of their store, she shifted to the vacant lot: one day it was white, bare, the next heavy green, thick with needled aroma like the mountains where Mrs. Orleski said her son worked deep in the Crowsnest Mines. I could not imagine that then, crows' nests were bundles of sticks notched high in poplars and a coal mine was. . . . When her son came home for one day at Christmas you could see the coal engrained in his skin like topsoil in the drifts of a three-day prairie blizzard. His shoulders had a hockey player's powerful slope and were only a little narrower than Oncle Willm's and he liked to show his favourite muscle, a bulge when he bent his elbow that heaved up and clenched itself rock-hard and not even Whipper Billy Watson the heavyweight wrestling champion of the world could muster that; he knew, for he had once challenged Watson and that dead-white mound of muscle from Toronto had backed off: nothing but the usual stuff in his arm.

"Jolly old St. Nicholas, lean your ear this way . . ." murmured the wall of the store. If Doerksen Brothers, Anni said, leaned any farther they would fall over.

"You kits still lookin'?" Mrs. Orleski pulled her hands from between her three summer coats and whatever else she wore underneath, sweaters and skirts and every kind of unmentionable. "Sell, lotsa sell this year, see," and she gestured around with her arms wide, a little stump of a fireplug turning as if about to break into dance. There were only three trees left, three scrunchy trees in a trampled scatter of spruce-tips and sodden snow; abruptly she wheeled and her nostrils flared into the chinook, opening hugely like gills in fast water, "Here, here! They leave it, the leetle branch, they leave it lotsa . . ." and she was stooping, gathering with the swift inevitable hands of workers, "Sometimes stump, have it too much branch . . ." and she thrust them at me, offering in the wimpling eddy off the sun-and-wind-warmed wall a stinging memory of motionless feathered muskeg, our black dog plunging head and tail through the crystalline velvet sinking of it, the indented spoors of rabbits and a slither of weasels: Mrs. Orleski's two stubby arms filled with spruce boughs like a proffered squirrel nest stuffed fat and full and warm for the winter, "You take it, is good, hang it some places, Mama happy so . . . ." Offering the wistful windy madness of a gift.

"I'm sorry," Anni said, and I stared at her in horror. "We still have no money."

"Wha? I no take it, your money . . . give for nutting, you, take!"

And I took and ran. Anni behind me argued, the very bend of her body declaring you cannot accept a gift from someone as poor as yourself and certainly not from anyone richer and so you refuse to accept anything from anyone, ever; and finally thanked the old lady, almost angrily as if forced and following me with her long legs scissoring through the last sunshine past the principal's yellow and green house and across the schoolyard. The little Japanese houses stood one by one along the south side of the street, their double windows with their pale never-opened blinds dreaming even in the long winter like unfathomable Buddhas. "It's Christmas, and anyway it cleans up her lot." But any word of mine just set Anni's teeth more visibly into her bottom lip, her head lower into the branches as if she would chew needles. Both her pails were stuck full, my basket was too small for all my armful but I didn't drop a twig all the way home and I slid neither flat nor flying in the mud either.

Old Ema Racht passed us, alone like a procession in his smoking Buick. In the rich darkness of the car his whiskers flared from the sides of his face like white flames reaching for the side windows as he drove without headlights, his arms braced rigid before him and his eyes peering ahead as if to illumine the fluid road with their glare. The chinook seeped spruce through my head; had I known about such things then I would have known I was at least drunk when I heaved up my branches, waved, shouted, "Froe Wiehnachte!" And his head turned to us trudging the shoulder of the road, heavily around like a spray of cannon wheeling and he saw me, his eyes briefly the driven ends of spikes, and the huge polished flank of the car lurched toward me as at a recognition before his head trundled back and cocked forward again on his long neck over the steering wheel and his stiff arms kept his shoulders rammed back against the seat and his beaked nose defied that lunatic wind, dared it to squirm him into the gumbo ditch, he would *not* turn that wheel, he would *not* raise either his right foot from the gas or his left foot from the clutch and so he roared away into the warm settling dusk of Christmas Eve, finally merging far ahead of us into the misty dinosaur legs of the bare cottonwoods surrounding his immense yard: an antediluvian monster roaring in futile and foehnish anthem the cacophonous wonders of the Christ-child season. Gifts upon gifts, the smell of gas and clutchplate snipped at our nostrils through the green of spruce till we saw the rectangular windows of our house stunned golden everyone with the vanished sun reflecting from the laden, burning bellies of the clouds, and the mud squishing under our feet and the prick of spruce on our cold wrists and fingers. I looked at Anni. Her hair streamed flat under wind, the cloven flames of window and sky glistened, blazed in her eyes.

"Don't say a word," she said.

And I did that. Even when I saw our father was already home because the dairy pick-up was parked beside our door, I said nothing. But once inside, oh, talk! Our house was packed tight with smells like nuts in a Christmas cake and we hung our branches singing everywhere until its two rooms seemed flung all over with a green and poignant spray. Then we stepped into the fresh darkness and the purring, dialed cab of the truck wafted us to church, a wide building where the men sat in two broad aisles on the right and the women in two aisles on the left and we children crammed in front directly under the benign (for tonight) faces of the ministers leaning over the pulpit and the choir curved around behind them, and we sang those Christmas songs our people had brought from half a world away, so out of place now in the treeless, flat irrigation prairies but not at all out of spirit:

"Leise rieselt der Schnee,
 Still und starr ruht der See;
 Weihnachtlich glaenzet der Wald,
 Freue dich, Christkind kommt bald!"

the high beautiful voices of the women, the deep heavy voices of the men, and the bright thread of my father's tenor between them where he sat behind me among rich farmers and storekeepers and workers and teachers and unemployed labourers. Two ministers spoke, very short and mostly stories, and there were several long prayers, and the choir sang, several children's groups sang, and then we all sang again,

"Nun is sie erschienen, die himmlische Sonne..."

and

"O Fest, aller heiligen Feste,
 O Weihnacht, du lieblicher Schein..."

and then young men came in with big boxes and gave every child a small brown bag which we were not allowed to open in church but we could so easily feel whether we had an orange or an apple and there was at least one chocolate bar and almost a whole handful of peanuts and either six or even seven candies, and then we sang,

"Stille Nacht, heilige Nacht
 Alles schlaeft, einsam wacht
 Nur das traute, hochheilige Paar,
 Das im Stalle zu Bethlehem war
 Bei dem himmlischen Kind,
 Bei dem himmlischen Kind."

And then without talking or running around we all went quickly and quietly home. No clouds now, the sky was brilliant, clear black with crystals of stars frozen over us, the air silent as a curtain: tomorrow would be very cold. And on our front step a small wooden box. I bumped against it as I jumped for the door trying to get in fast to see whether I had an O Henry or a Sweet Marie in my bag.

The board squeaked up—what was that? Those are oranges, my father said, Japanese oranges. They can be eaten. Roundly moist in their pale wrappers, they unzipped themselves under his fingernail symmetrically with a strange, sharp sweetness like regular little oriental shelves opening. Who could have left them for us? Such a vividly useless gift, all you could do was eat it. So we did: Anni and I each ate nine.

Then my father read, as he always did, from "And there went out a decree from Caesar Augustus . . ." all the way to where the shepherds returned to their flocks glorifying and praising God, and then we each said a very short prayer with the house so quiet now I could hear the coal shift as it burned in the stove and Anni and I placed our plates—like always the very biggest we could find—on the kitchen table under the spruce branches all ready for the gifts we knew we would get from the "Nate Klous"—always useful gifts like toothbrushes or socks or a shirt at most—and then we climbed up the narrow stairs to our two small rooms with a final, tenth, Japanese shelving itself lingeringly into our mouths.

"Who was it?" Anni asked, breathing orange in the darkness.

I said, "Who knows?" But I did. I knew it as certainly as a child knows everything at Christmas. As certainly as the hard clear sanity of the north wind's song beginning at the window, and in my ear, our little house I believe swaying gently like a cradle, very, very gently.

The House Smashers

Edmonton's first mayor was a Conservative named Matt McCauley, and its first federal cabinet minister Frank Oliver—a Liberal, believe it or not. Now they've named a skyscraper-shopping centre after the one and a town with a big mental hospital after the other, but in my time they were best known for being convicted house smashers.

It was about the time the CPR didn't come to Edmonton, a few winters before the Louis Riel scare on the Saskatchewan. One warm Saturday in February an American named L. George drove stakes at the corners of a river lot east of where the Macdonald Hotel now stands and before anyone noticed much had, with several men he hired, put up a rail fence and started building a house. The lot was two hundred yards wide and ran north from the river up over the high bank and all of two miles back to Rat Creek: a very nice bit of land if you could get it by knocking up a hundred-dollar shack.

"Well, have you got title to it?" L. George hollered from behind some two-by-fours he was holding for his carpenter.

"You know nobody's got title, only the Bay Reserve's been surveyed yet!" McCauley yelled back.

"So go . . ." and L. George gestured, turned to hammering again.

That night he set up a tent on the wooden floor and slept in it. Sunday in Edmonton, then, was always a day for church and restful thought; a pondering of life and its possible meanings. Sunday night was very cold, but early Monday morning L. George emerged from his tent and soon was sawing with all his hired help. Sleighs and pedestrians kept passing in the snow ruts of Jasper Avenue—as they'd just renamed Main Street; many of them were men who had bought small expensive lots west on Jasper from the Bay, and others men who had lived there for ten, twelve years and always believed that the land on which they built their businesses and homes would surely be theirs when the government finally got surveyors out of central Ontario as far west as the North Saskatchewan River valley. But if this American had discovered a new way, and the North-West Mounted Police continued to have nothing to say about land, why, someone who looked like Frank Oliver was heard to mutter, "Let the facts be known at once so that shotgun law can prevail."

The sun was low in the winter sky. More men gathered to inspect the new building, and they did not leave. When one loud voice requested that somebody better get his goddam shack outa there, L. George put down his hammer and drew a large revolver from his carpenter's apron. By this time the brittle rail fence had disappeared, and one of the several hundred men milling about slipped behind L. George and grabbed him while someone else deprived him of his revolver. The carpenters now picked up their tools and left; hands were reaching everywhere for L. George, and the only reason he remained in the building was because he was being assisted to leave it between so many different studs at the same time. But then ropes arrived, and the building began to move south toward the river bank.

There were some problems. The bank is two hundred feet high at this point, more or less straight down, and the tent and bed were removed but still the building hesitated; it merely teetered. Then L. George stepped out and the building lost its balance, fell, bounced down in more and more pieces until it spread itself over a small patch of frozen river. The rest of the lumber went flying after it, and then L. George accepted his revolver back.

I think only Matt McCauley and Frank Oliver were ever tried for smashing that house. One was pure Conservative, the other pure Liberal, and for some reason they walked into Inspector Gagnon's NWMP office together just when L. George was filing damages there for ten thousand dollars and they were both immediately arrested, with complete political impartiality. There were two dozen witnesses ready to swear they had seen both of them with their hands on ropes, on corner studs just before the house fell; Oliver had even been heard verbally encouraging others in similar acts. So Gagnon committed them for trial in June. They were convicted with overwhelming evidence, fined a dollar each, and in October the surveyors arrived from Ottawa.

A dollar was worth a lot in those days, sure, but I still think McCauley and Oliver were lucky. Sir John A. might have sent an English general after them. I mean, Louis Riel tried to get surveys and land titles for thousands of people who had been living on the prairies for generations, and you know what happened to him? They hanged him. And they haven't named a mental hospital after him yet.

The road through Hastings' Farm, Duffield, traverses the
gently rolling hills of the Lake Wabamun area, west of
Edmonton.

Opposite: South tower of the Edmonton Centre, one of the
many new buildings that have transformed downtown
Edmonton during the past decade.

Above: Faithful fans watch the Edmonton Eskimos play the
Calgary Stampeders at the Commonwealth Stadium during the
1978 Western Final—in a temperature of −25°C.

Marmot Basin, Jasper, is one of the finest skiing and hiking
areas in the national parks.

A ptarmigan camouflaged for winter.

Opposite: As described in the story "Lake Isle of Innisfree," a generous financier built this beautiful bank for the residents of the picturesque little town because the surrounding countryside reminded him of his home.

Above: Chester Ronning, the distinguished China diplomat, stands in front of "Old Main" at the Camrose Lutheran College, which as a young man he helped to build and later ran as one of the province's most progressive educators.

Upper: Winter with a smile.

Lower: A camel ponders December at the Alberta Game Farm.

Upper: The school bus is a familiar sight on the back roads of Alberta.

Lower: A less familiar sight is the mammoth *pysanky* at Vegreville—witness to the predominantly Ukrainian-Canadian population of the town.

Upper: The coldest days are often the most beautiful.

Lower: Tosca by the Edmonton Opera Society, 1978.

Opposite: This view of Edmonton from the Cloverdale Flats shows the embankment over which the offending shack was cast in the story of "The House Smashers."

Opposite: A rig west of Buck Mountain is part of the
development of the massive oil and natural gas reserves
discovered along the eastern edge of the Rocky Mountains.

Above: Fenceline and drifts near Lethbridge.

Opposite: The "end of the line" at Mountain Park, once a
thriving mining community.

Above: The town of Coleman owes its existence to coal
deposits in the area and to the construction of the Canadian
Pacific Railway, which runs through the town to British
Columbia, via the Crowsnest Pass.

Above: Cross-country skiing—on the North Saskatchewan
River, near Edmonton.

Opposite: Elbow Falls, in the foothills of the Rockies,
southwest of Calgary.

High winds sweep the eastern slopes of the Rocky Mountains
near Cadomin.

A History of the New World

Box 3,
Indiana, Alta. T0A 1Z0

July 30

Dear Professor.
You asked to write down my Opinion, to write makes Things clearer, so I will tell you I have read Thousands of Books of all sorts. Some of them Were just Picking up Here and there, what we may call collage, to me that is ZERO. Books like you talk about for me, a free thinker, have no purpose or goal toward light and truth. Religion believers have lost the original goal of Civilization

  = the Conquest of Man by itself with no God, no master
  = doing the Right Thing because it is Right
  = with no fear of God or the Devil as a way to attain Beatitude.

You look at the pictures on my wall and my book piles and ask if I am a Socialist. I am a lot worse than that, and in Alberta that Something. Religions (3000 in the World) have given the Ignoramus a way of life. He can avoid developing his Human potential. If you have Religion given to you, by Baptism or other Hoodoo Worship, it makes no difference, the development of the grey matter cease at 27 years old when the bones of the Cranium solidify. Finish: no more growing.

If, for instance, a person has had the misfortune to be Baptize in Religion, the bones of the FONTANEL are solidly welded together, then if in some way his Brain Waken in a splurge of Energy, *he die instantly*. And that no b.s. It happen every day and they call that a stroke.

I am one of the fortunate individuals that was blessed with a Human being for a father. A man at 8 years who was on the barricade in 1871 Commune in Paris, who worked at that age = 14 hours a day for 20 cents with his two Brothers in a Brickplant. My father at 27 was the bodyguard of old Clemenceau, the Tiger of France, and also secretary of the Radical Socialist Movement. But being primordially HONEST, He did not climb the ladder of Politic. At 6 years old He used to take me to political meetings with the Idea that to be a Citizen you start Early.

When I was 14 years old I wrote a Book in a week, 500 pages. "The History of the new World." That was so far advanced in Thoughts that friends of my father told me to destroy it as nobody would believe that a kid 14 could write it. I could do that because Thinking is Electric phenomenon with waves like Radio that never stop through the universe ad Infinitum. The thinker open himself to the Telepathic message: we think when we are open to thoughts and lost in the Dim past we have quadrillions of ancestors, making a liar of any man proclaiming himself "Self Made Man."

Sincerely yours for the Golden Rule—the
only law for Real Peace
Jean Labarge

A 88 year old Philosopher graduate in
the University of Hard Knocks

University of Calbridge,

October 11

Dear Mr. Labarge:
I'm sorry to be so long answering your letter, but my summer was full of travel and...well, your letters are made to ponder. I have a wonderful memory of you standing in your magnificent garden, so far north and the July corn already up to your shoulder and even the horse radish knee-high, growing on the soil you made yourself from lake sand and wood ashes (Did you buy that pike the little boy offered, and ran? I'm surprised you don't fish yourself, the lake lapping your land, though if those terrified little boys will sell them for fifty cents I suppose it's not worth the bother): I can only think of you as a French gourmet who grows all the ingredients for his vegetarian feasts himself.

But you are also a free-thinker, and if so you must be open to any experience that will enlighten you and your comprehension of the world. Now we all believe something; even you, who believe in the Golden Rule. It strikes me that Jesus lived that Rule (he stated it better than anyone) as well as anyone in history ever has, so your argument against Christian believers (since you mention baptism) cannot be with *him*: it must be with the way his teachings have been abused, right? So why do you throw him out with all "Hoodoo worshippers"? That's not free-thinking. That's like throwing out Mao because some of his followers are ignorant killers.

Also, I cannot follow you on "the goal of civilization." Our western "civilization" is one of many developments in history. What common goal could the disparate (a pun if you like) millions of the world have unless it were one given to them by the creator who started the whole matter of universe in the first place? You may call that "creator" anything you please (and don't throw any "six-day-creation" dust at me either) but surely a free-thinker would be the first to recognize that the primordial slime out of which our ancestors, presumably, crawled, the primordial thought which somehow (as you have it) has us all thinking, they must have originated somewhere. In other words, something was; *before* we began. It could not have been *Nothing*.

I can never pretend I am "free" in any absolute sense of that word: I am tied to a body, to gravity, to psychic and mental demands and limits—demands and limits both hereditary and environmental and volitional. I often have no comprehension where these limits come from, and even when I know I can do little to resolve them. Oh, I am free to think what I please, certainly, but actually I am hemmed in even there by a limited (conditioned, uninformed?) imagination. In what sense is anyone, ever, a *free* thinker? It seemed to me you were, for example, hemmed in by your hatred of Calgary Power, a hatred perhaps justified since their engineers dug up the street and then filled it so badly that contaminated water seeped through and soured your root cellar and so destroyed all your carrots; hemmed in by your fear that the town boys would tear up your garden (if you curse them every time they walk by, what can you expect?); even hemmed in by your long-set refusal to consider religious options which millions of people have, over the centuries, found gave them peace and a certain uneasy happiness. I have given up pretending I can ever be free; my freedom I believe must consist in what I commit myself to and that . . . .

Indiana, Alta.

Oct. 14

Dear profess.

A free man live with his Brain and Exist with his Stomach. I did not read the end of your letter because I know it Already.

I came to Canada in 1910 because the Canada Immigration covered France with paper that anybody could make $10,000 in five years, just work hard to make a farm. So I come to Edmonton, $400 and I could have bought a Whole block of Jasper Avenue but those papers say Farm and I bought three oxen with $400 and started walking North on the Grouard Trail. There was land by the Section there they said, and lots of French. And lots of Priests too, they didn't say. Started June 6, 1910, and got to Grouard on Lesser Slave Lake Sept. 13, 1910, walk every Step and one Ox sank in a swamp trying to get away from Mosquitoes, the second ran home—only time he ever move that fast, I have to walk to Edmonton three years later to get him, all summer Trip, and the only one Ox left so thin he was not even edible. I farm at Grouard, McLennan, High Prairie, Girouxville, all over 45 years, and then I got Smashed in a car accident and sold the farm: $6000 and the lawyer take $2000 for fee. That's the Canada Immigration Farm Dream. How rich would I be with two blocks on Jasper Avenue beside the Hudsons Bay, eh? Goddam capitalist, and that's no b.s. Thank god and Jesus and the virgin, if you want, I live from Ground I Made myself, I got so little I can shoot anybody wants to grab it, and I give you peas again if you come stand in my gate and talk. They're still growing, but I have to cover them every night.

You sent me a Good picture. Your nice wife knows More about gardens than you, but you know it Already.

Altogether during 1000 years of the Dark Age over 50 millions of European peoples were murdered in the name of the Cross and Jesus Christ. In 1979 years now the Atomic and Hydrogen and Neutron Bomb, Bio warfare, etc. All done with the rejoicing of all religions: a very Christian future of Peace on Earth.

> Total writing time = 13 minutes.
> It is crazy to worry
> fifty below rain or shine
> Silly enough to be Happy
> to Enjoy life is no Crime

NOTE = the grey matter of Brains has enough power to push out the bones of the Cranium ad Infinitum
To the Seeker for Know How, there is no limit. Try it.

j.l.

Growing Up in Rosebud

In 1896 when I first went to school in a log building near Rosebud, we often saw men fighting over politics. You know, grown men knocking each other down if they could, or at least breaking a few teeth. Whenever the Conservatives were getting the worst of it, one of us little Conservatives would run for the North-West Mounted Police constable. The Liberals that year had made up a song for school kids to sing, and when any of them sang it we were supposed to start fighting too. I never did. I thought Frank Oliver, who became minister of the interior in Laurier's cabinet, looked far more impressive than the Conservative candidate, but my dad said Oliver just had that huge, droopy moustache so you couldn't tell which side of his mouth he was talking out of and when they sang,

> "Oliver rides on a big white horse,
> Cochrane on a mule.
> Oliver is a gentleman,
> And Cochrane is a fool,"

I better start swinging or I'd explain myself to him behind our barn. So whenever I heard the song begin I was always swinging as I high-tailed for Rosebud Coulee.

The nearest polling station was at Elliot's, west of Carbon about twenty miles from our place, but my dad said he had to go and vote even though it would take him almost two days to get there and back. I bumped along on the wagon with him and I remember the Conservative scrutineer at the booth, though I won't mention his name. He'd say to anyone who looked him straight in the eye, "See Angus in the barn." Angus was taking care of good Conservatives there, and he took care of my dad so well that I drove the team home all the way while he lay in the bottom of the wagon box and watched the stars and sang songs I had never heard before and didn't again for quite a while after. Politics were more important then, I think.

My mother was the local medicine woman. She had learned a lot from the Indians about herbs and roots, and always had a big bag of them hanging behind the stove. If you had a sore that wouldn't heal, you came to her and she'd take out a root, chew it, and tie the mash tight over the sore. I never knew whether it was the root or my mother's spit, but the sores always healed. She even healed my dad when he spent three days in a snowdrift in January 1907.

The Indian weatherman told him not to go, the low heavy haze in the north looked bad, but the sun was bright and he started north, thirty-five miles to my uncle's. When the blizzard hit we thought he had probably stopped at a ranch, but he was in a snowdrift ten miles away and for three days lived on flour and snow. After a while he thought he heard voices, that all around him in the drift were the people he knew and they were calling to him. So he was still alive when the storm was over and he found his horses frozen solid to the sleigh and started to walk home. But his feet were so frozen they wouldn't carry him. He rested and crawled, rested and crawled until he saw the banks of Rosebud Creek near our house in the setting sun, but he was too weak by then to lift his head. He lay down to die and suddenly a strong voice told him to get up. The sun had gone down, but he felt stronger then and he crawled a little farther to the top of a hill, and my mother who had been looking out the window all day, praying, saw the dark object in the snow and told me to go see what it was. So I found my dad and carried him home.

After a while there was nothing wrong with him but his feet. When his toes started to rot, my mother held the butcher knife and I hit it clean and sharp with the hammer, once for each toe and that fixed him. She healed him up otherwise, but he could just wear moccasins after that. He died in the General Hospital in Calgary twenty-two years later.

The Funny Money of 1980

I never wanted to be a politician, least of all premier of Alberta. I refused to accept a nomination in the election of 1935, but when the Social Credit League swept fifty-six of sixty-three seats (there were entire polls where not a single vote was cast for United Farmer or Liberal or Conservative candidates), every one of our elected members offered to resign if I would accept the leadership. I always considered that election to be my call from God through the voice of the people and was premier until my death, almost eight years later. May 23, 1943. And now most Albertans know little more about me than some faint whiff of "fire and brimstone" preaching, of "funny money," of. . . .

There is no need to defend my record. If my leadership of this province during its greatest crisis is seen as a deviation, a disorder of standard politics, then I say "Hallelujah!" Standard politics had almost destroyed us by 1935, and there is a real danger in the 1980s that they will do so again. Listen, listen to me and—in my day I never had to tell people twice to listen. I stood six foot two, weighed an eighth of a ton, and on the windiest Alberta day I never needed a microphone to get the biggest crowd's attention. "Mr. Aberhart," all those frank, weathered faces begged me, "tell us the truth." And I did.

Albertans in 1980 are like a man making a journey into a strange country. Towards the end of a beautiful day—the finest he has any memory of—he comes to a crossing where five roads meet. He is aware suddenly of the sun sinking, that the hills into which the roads disappear are covered with heavy night clouds, but ahh, there is a guidepost—fallen to the ground! Five directions, how will he ever find his destination? After pondering for a time, he asks himself, "What do I know that will guide me? I know which road I came by, and where I came from." And with that he picks up the guidepost, turns it until the correct marker points in the direction from which he came, and immediately he knows the destination of the four other roads.

In case you weren't here, or have forgotten, let me tell you where Alberta came from. In 1930 it was the most desperately poor province in all of Canada because it had been settled last, very quickly, and its people had borrowed enormous sums against the land in order to buy machinery to work it. When Depression wheat dropped to twenty cents a bushel, hogs to two cents a pound, it was impossible to pay ten percent mortgages: life became a war and Albertans lost everything. Do you know how many of our young men were rejected for the army in 1939 because they had rickets from malnutrition? I know, and that's only the men; no one bothered to count the women and children.

There was starvation in Alberta not because the land would not produce. The coal was always in the ground, the wheat always grew to an extent (there was never total drought in all areas), but the mine owners allowed only enough coal production to keep prices up; mortgage companies had taken the land and the machinery away from farmers, so how could they farm? People starved while wheat rotted in storage, was dumped into the sea to keep consumer prices high. Because Big Money always protects its investment.

You think many rich people became paupers after the crash of '29? Let me tell you, they were paper millionaires to begin with, their supposed wealth based on the speculation numbers of a speculative stock market. Those who actually owned land and resources, the Rockefellers, the Masseys, the J. Paul Gettys, became richer than ever during the Depression, and distillers like the Bronfmans who prey on human beings in misery joined them in a luxury unknown to the wealthiest kings of antiquity. Have you heard of a single Canadian bank, a single brewery that went broke in the thirties? You could look forever. Their money power controlled our country, and it was stronger than the elected power of the people because the traditional political parties were under the Big Money thumbs too. Private enterprise had been allowed to expand far beyond the public good, and that is wrong, wrong! So, when our Social Credit government passed revolutionary legislation that would have put rightful power back in the hands of the people, the Supreme Court of Canada, never once speaking to the issues we tackled, simply ruled our legislation *ultra vires*, "beyond provincial competence" because its judges of course were Big Money people too. We starved until Hitler attacked Poland, and then suddenly, at the first shot of a gun, we were wealthy enough to fight the most expensive war in history—why? Because Big Money knows that the biggest profits of all are made by blowing people up! So they let us produce again, as we could have all along.

Ohhh, when I think of it I am so enraged I could pray for the wrath of God to flame down from heaven and—but I wanted to set up the guidepost for my beloved province in 1980.

I want to ask you one question: Is it possible that Alberta, with the exploitation of its marvellous natural resources, is becoming like one of the propertied rich of the Depression? It allows Middle East potentates and monopoly oil companies to set unbelievably high oil prices and then says to its fellow Canadian consumers, "Well, you'll have to pay because that's the world price, now isn't it. Sorry." Windfall profits, profits that for the most part have nothing to do with legitimate earnings: profits at the expense, the exploitation of the general public. Well, does Alberta at least use these enormous profits to help people; for example, encourage research in new methods of conservation, to experiment with more efficient production and distribution of food to the world's starving, to say nothing of aiding refugees in their flight from oppression and misery? Have you heard anything about that? No. Instead, taxation on the big foreign oil companies is eased so that they can increase their gigantic profits even more quickly. At the same time, school and hospital budgets are cut by inflation and the poor and unemployed people increase all over the province. Alberta has the highest divorce *and* suicide rate in Canada, why? Because wherever the rich and fortunate cluster, there also the social contrast is greatest and the unsuccessful are driven to the greatest despair.

What do Albertans really want with their enormous wealth? The temporary (resource wealth is *always* temporary) satisfaction of standing at the top of the sandpile and thumbing their noses at the rest of Canada and chanting, "Haha on you, we're on top! We've got the money, now we'll call the politics!"? I cannot believe we are so childish.

If our memory of the Depression is any kind of guide at all, it should teach us that the people of Alberta *deserve* their present wealth no more than the people of Alberta deserved their Depression poverty. We have had some good resource management in the past, but resource wealth is a gift oh so easily squandered; it is the business of a democratic people to elect those to leadership who will use and build on those gifts wisely: for the wider human good. If they do not, they will soon suffer for it, together with their short-sighted politicians.

And if this sounds a lot like a sermon, don't be surprised. I was a preacher much longer than I was a politician; or have been dead. Do not be deceived by a fleeting prosperity. Let me assure you, there is a larger and ultimate justice that rules the world, both the living and the so-called dead.

Opposite: A lumber truck passes through Caroline. This once quiet little town is now part of the hustle and bustle of resource development on the eastern slopes of the Rockies.

Above: Spring opens up the foothills country along the road to Water Valley.

Marshall Wells store, Cereal. The town's name is a reflection of the fine crops grown in the district.

A lone sign marks what was once the town of Majestic. Only the sign remains.

The N. D. Café at New Dayton is one of the innumerable Chinese restaurants found in small towns across the prairies.

Ferry at Dorothy. Each year, more of the few remaining ferries are taken out of service.

Alpine meadows near Angel Glacier on Mount Edith Cavell. The mountain was given its present name in honour of the famous World War I nurse. In the fur-trading days it was known as La Montagne de la Grande Traverse, since it lay between the Athabasca and Columbia river systems.

Mountain sheep. In the spring months many species of wildlife can be seen along the highways in Jasper National Park as the animals wait for the snows to melt in the high country.

Above: The Valley of the Ten Peaks in Banff National Park
was once known as Desolation Valley. At the foot of these
imposing peaks lies the beautiful Moraine Lake.

Opposite: The rugged country which towers above Sentinel
Pass makes this part of Banff National Park a hiker's paradise.

Young barley pushes up through the soil at Bellis during that
all-too-brief time of year when the prairie turns emerald.

Boy Scouts and Girl Guides belt out a tune at the Ukrainian
Pioneer Village, east of Edmonton.

Moss grows along a mountain stream
in the back country above Kootenay Plains.

Perennial flower garden, Hardisty. All across the province,
thousands of small gardens bear colourful witness to the spirit
of the early settler.

Near Dog Pound, a mare and her foal bask in the long-awaited
first days of spring. This area was a favourite wintering place
for the Indian people.

Recess in the schoolyard, near Venice. The town was named by
the community's first postmaster who arrived from Venice,
Italy, in 1902.

Marsh marigolds sparkle in the sun at Athabasca Landing.

A farm at Cremona, near the foot of the Rockies, marks the
end of the arable land and the beginning of timber.

Early morning calm, Waterton Lakes National Park. Situated
in the southwest corner of the province, the park is a haven
for those who enjoy peace and quiet in a magnificent setting.

This Greek Orthodox church lies in the mixed farming country around Wasel. The church onion domes are a common feature of the region.

Old-timers, Lethbridge.

Gently rolling farmlands in central Alberta.

The Angel of the Tar Sands

Spring had most certainly, finally, come. The morning drive to the plant from Fort McMurray was so dazzling with fresh green against the heavy spruce, the air so unearthly bright that it swallowed the smoke from the candy-striped chimneys as if it did not exist. Which is just lovely, the superintendent thought, cut out all the visible crud, shut up the environmentalists, and he went into his neat office (with the river view with islands) humming, "Alberta blue, Alberta blue, the taste keeps—" but did not get his tan golfing jacket off before he was interrupted. Not by the radio-telephone, by Tak the day operator on Number Two Bucket in person, walking past the secretary without stopping.

"What the hell?" the superintendent said, quickly annoyed.

"I ain't reporting this on no radio," Tak's imperturbable Japanese-Canadian face was tense, "if them reporters hear about this one they—"

"You scrape out *another* buffalo skeleton, for god's sake?"

"No, it's maybe a dinosaur this time, one of them—"

But the superintendent, swearing, was already out the door yelling for Bertha who was always on stand-by now with her spade. If one of the three nine-storey-high bucketwheels stopped turning for an hour the plant dropped capacity, but another archaeological leak could stop every bit of production for a month while bifocalled professors stuck their noses. . . . The jeep leaped along the track beside the conveyor belt running a third empty already and in three minutes he had Bertha with her long-handled spade busy on the face of the fifty-foot cliff that Number Two had been gnawing out. A shape emerged, quickly.

"What the. . ." staring, the superintendent could not find his ritual words, ". . . is that?"

"When the bucket hit the corner of it," Tak said, "I figured hey, that's the bones of a—"

"That's not just bone, it's. . .skin and. . . ." The superintendent could not say the word.

"Wings," Bertha said it for him, digging her spade in with steady care. "That's wings, like you'd expect on a angel."

For that's what it was, plain as the day now, tucked tight into the oozing black cliff, an angel. Tak had seen only a corner of bones sheared clean but now that Bertha had it more uncovered they saw the manlike head through one folded-over pair of wings and the manlike legs, feet through another pair, very gaunt, the film of feathers and perhaps skin so thin and engrained with tarry sand that at first it was impossible to notice anything except the white bones inside them. The third pair of wings was pressed flat by the sand at a very awkward, it must have been painful—

"The middle two," Bertha said, trying to brush the sticky sand aside with her hand, carefully, "is what it flies with."

"Wouldn't it . . . he . . . fly with all six . . . six . . . ." The superintendent stopped, overwhelmed by the unscientific shape uncovered there so blatantly.

"You can look it up," Bertha said with a sideways glance at his ignorance, "Isaiah chapter six."

But then she gagged too for the angel had moved. Not one of them was touching it, that was certain, but it had moved irrefutably. As they watched, stunned, the wings unfolded bottom and top, a head emerged, turned, and they saw the fierce hoary lineaments of an ancient man. His mouth all encrusted with tar pulled open and out came a sound. A long, throat-clearing streak of sound. They staggered back, fell; the superintendent found himself on his knees staring up at the shape which wasn't really very tall, it just seemed immensely broad and overwhelming, the three sets of wings now sweeping back and forth as if loosening up in some seraphic 5BX plan. The voice rumbled like thunder, steadily on.

"Well," muttered Tak, "whatever it is, it sure ain't Japanese."

The superintendent suddenly saw himself as an altar boy, the angel suspended above him there and bits of words rose to his lips: "*Pax vobis . . . cem . . . cum*," he ventured, but the connections were lost in the years, "*Magnifi . . . cat . . . ave Mar . . . .*"

The obsidian eyes of the angel glared directly at him and it roared something, dreadfully. Bertha laughed aloud.

"Forget the popish stuff," she said. "It's talking Hutterite, Hutterite German."

"Wha . . . ." The superintendent had lost all words; he was down to syllables only.

"I left the colony. . . ." But then she was too busy listening. The angel kept on speaking, non-stop as if words had been plugged up inside for eons, and its hands (it had only two of them, in the usual place at the ends of two arms) brushed double over its bucket-damaged shoulder and that appeared restored, whole just like the other, while it brushed the soil and tarry sand from its wings, flexing the middle ones again and again because they obviously had suffered much from their position.

"Ber . . . Ber . . ." the superintendent said. Finally he looked at Tak, pleading for a voice.

"What's it saying," Tak asked her, "Bertha, please Bertha?"

She was listening with overwhelming intensity; there was nothing in this world but to hear. Tak touched her shoulder, shook her, but she did not notice. Suddenly the angel stopped speaking; it was studying her.

"I . . . I can't . . . ." Bertha confessed to it at last, "I can understand every word you . . . every word, but I can't say, I've forgotten . . . ."

In its silence the angel looked at her; slowly its expression changed. It might have been showing pity, though of course that is really difficult to tell with angels. Then it folded its lower wings over its feet, its upper wings over its face, and with an ineffable movement of its giant middle wings it rose, straight upward into the blue sky. They bent back staring after it, and in a moment it had vanished in light.

"O dear god," Bertha murmured after a time. "Our Elder always said they spoke Hutterite in heaven."

They three contemplated each other and they saw in each other's eyes the dread, the abrupt tearing sensation of doubt. Had they seen . . . and as one they looked at the sand cliff still oozing tar, the spade leaning against it. Beside the hole where Bertha had dug: the shape of the angel, indelible. Bertha was the first to get up.

"I quit," she said. "Right this minute."

"Of course, I understand." The superintendent was on his feet. "Tak, run your bucket through there, get it going quick."

"Okay," Tak said heavily. "You're the boss."

"It doesn't matter how fast you do it," Bertha said to the superintendent but she was watching Tak trudge into the shadow of the giant wheel, "it was there, we saw it."

And at her words the superintendent had a vision. He saw like an opened book the immense curves of the Athabasca River swinging through wilderness down from the glacial pinnacles of the mountains and across Alberta and joined by the Berland and the McLeod and the Pembina and the Pelican and the Christina and the Clearwater and the Firebag rivers, and all the surface of the earth was gone, the Tertiary and the Lower Cretaceous layers of strata had been ripped away and the thousands of square miles of black bituminous sand were exposed, laid open, slanting down into the molten centre of the earth, O *miserere, miserere,* the words sang in his head and he felt their meaning though he could not have explained them, much less remembered Psalm 51, and after a time he could open his eyes and lift his head. The huge plant, he knew every bolt and pipe, still sprawled between him and the river; the brilliant air still swallowed the smoke from all the red-striped chimneys as if it did not exist, and he knew that through a thousand secret openings the oil ran there, gurgling in each precisely numbered pipe and jointure, sweet and clear like golden brown honey.

Tak was beside the steel ladder, about to start the long climb into the machine. Bertha touched his shoulder and they both looked up.

"Next time you'll recognize it," she said happily. "And then it'll talk Japanese."

The Darkness Inside
the Mountain

Number Three Highway west of Lethbridge, paved, leads through Fort Macleod where at seven-thirty in the morning the black Hutterite men are already swinging off their staked cattle truck in front of the New American Café—"To buy ice-cream cones till the back door of the beer parlour opens," Daddy tells me, laughing—and then there's the high prairie of the Piegan Indian Reserve—"Watch for Horse-drawn Vehicles"—and in the emptiness against the foothills a tree has been set up. It couldn't have grown there so thick and all alone, its huge sawn-off branches holding up what at that distance looks like a platform of branches and blankets.

"That's the way they bury them," Daddy says. "Chiefs. High for the crows."

"Crows?" I can see one flapping across the summer shimmer of heat already buckling the hills.

"It's okay, better to fly off than be dragged deeper by worms."

That was one reason Mama didn't want me to go with him all day on his truck run to the Crowsnest Pass. "A girl of ten, Wendell, doesn't need *soaking* in cynicism." "Don't 'Wendell' me." "I didn't give you your name." "You don't have to use it, 'you' is enough." So I am in the red Coca-Cola truck he has driven since spring, bottles leaping in their crates when he can't miss a pothole, the mountains south of Pincher Creek like broken teeth with very bad fillings. The three Cowley elevators drone past, then Lundbreck with half-boarded-up square store fronts—"There's no mine here now, not even a saw-mill"—and the pavement ends with a crash and slither of gravel, the bottles going crazy. The railroad bounces doubly under us and against a hill, curves, and suddenly the road silence of a bridge, and thunder. Spray in clouds between cut rock—

"Daddy! Daddy!"

"Yeah, Lundbreck Falls. We'll have a look coming back."

They are gone behind an inevitable shoulder of rock and I'll have to wait with a memory of water hanging like brushed grey corduroy, vivid grey, not like irrigation falls, and the quick flash of rapids between trees and rocks, a shimmer spreading behind my eyelids as I squeeze them shut. When I open them there is the smoking cone of the Burmis sawmill but a tiny church also, you'd have to bend to go in, and over a hump the peaked and mortared stone walls of a—no, surely a castle! With all the wooden core of it burned out by a year-long siege, don't tell me!—and I look at Daddy and he doesn't, just grins and gestures ahead to the sudden upthrust of Crowsnest Mountain. Straight down the highway, over the narrow railroad track that cuts the gravel at right angles in front of Bellevue slouched on little hills ahead. We have to stop there while a string of mine cars tugs across.

"You must be good luck," Daddy says. "I never seen them going down the mine before."

Past our broad red nose the little cars are now all seated tight with blackish men facing each other knee to knee, hip-roofed lunch buckets in their laps. Each single giant monster eye on the top of each head turns, stares, and one by one they slide into the hole in the hillside, click *click*, click *click*, box after box of them slipping past where the sunlight of the trees and the blue sky stops like a wall. And for one instant that single eye glares from the darkness, and is gone, click *click,* click *click.*

The sun sits on the eastern mountains and I would like to curl up, arrange all this behind my eyelids, there is too much already, how can I possibly remember it all, but Bellevue is there, old stores cut into hillsides and a Chinese café and a Ukrainian café with bottle cases stacked in cellars, behind gaping fences, crashing as my father heaves them about single-handedly and the blackish faces of the off-work miners leaning across the porch rail of the Bellevue Hotel swivel with us as our long red truck flashes past in the window behind them. We bend around a large grey school and the road splits, straight ahead or down into the valley to a scatter of houses across the river and around a green hill. We drive straight on.

"What about those?"

"There's nobody there," Daddy says, "in Hillcrest, there's nothing there now."

Behind my eyelids I can see one of those little houses, look inside its one large room, and there is no ear to hear it as slowly, without a sound, the floor crashes soundlessly into the dark hole of the cellar below and the corners of black begin to move—I jerk my eyes open and a girl, tiny like me, tilts against the iron fence of the schoolyard with her hands up as if wired there and I wave, she is the first girl I have seen and I wave with both hands, desperately, but she does not move. Her face is early-summer brown like mine but she does not even blink, only her head turns like a mechanism and then we are plunging into the pale limestone wilderness of the Frank Slide under the ruptured face of Turtle Mountain. The highway and the railroad so smooth over and through it, a monumental cemetery for eighty people buried in two minutes; 1903, Daddy says, and on the edge of it they found a baby still sleeping in its cradle untouched. Through piled fields of boulders and past a store beside Gold Creek and then Turtle Mountain Playgrounds, and we stop in the noon shadow of that threatening overhang to eat sandwiches. Last night my mother packed them, and we wash their dryness down with Coca-Cola ice cold because my father exchanges two of our extras for cold bottles from the cooler inside.

"See that man," he says, chewing. "He's starting on his third million."

A slim man—he has arms, legs just like anyone, how could you see he is rich?—opens the door of a silvery-green convertible for a thinner woman with hair like a cloud of gold piled upon her head. O, she is. Rich. The convertible murmurs, spins away, their heads leaning back together, they almost touch.

"He was just born," my father says, "that's how he got all that."

Blairmore is one long street facing lower green mountains, the

CPR station, and the water tower. And a longer alley black with heat and the fried stink of food, the blackness moving, settling, settling down like granular snow in the blistering day, everywhere. I sort bottles, my hands like the miners' faces but sticky with pop too, and my father stacks cases five-high and hauls them in and out, up and down on the two-wheeled dolly until finally we drive the length of the street again, bumping through the sunken sewer ditches that cross in front of every business and past green mine timbers squared up like tunnels on the cinder space beside the railroad—"Welcome to the 52nd Annual Mine Rescue Games"—and finally, finally, there is air at the open window and only the grainy blue of Crowsnest Mountain. By itself like a blessing, and the road folded left and upward in green arcs toward Coleman. My father is sweating; his thick hands shake as he rides back and forth through his ten gears into the hills.

"I can't work a whole day on that horse-p—." He gestures behind him but looks straight ahead. "Not such a killer day."

I had never thought he could. After three grocery and one drug store, four cafés, the Miners' Clubs and the Canadian Legion, he pulls up tight against the bright shade of the alley behind the hotel—"Take a rest, I won't be long"—and is gone. I lock the doors, stretch out and fall into sleep that breaks in sweat, I am gasping on the sweat-hot seat. I pull myself loose, clamber out and up, hand and toe up to the top of the cases on the truck. The bottles burn my fingers. And I cannot open them anyway like my father does by levering two caps together because my hands are far too small, and weak.

"I'll open one for you." A whiskered man, grey, his layers of clothing so black with dirt they shine below me in the terrific sun. He reaches up, his horned, gleaming hand takes one bottle from me and his lips draw back on his teeth and he places the top of the bottle there and at one slight grind of his head the hot liquid boils out between his whiskers and over his chin and down his layered front, but he does not notice. Just spits out the cap and looks up at me easily, offering me the hissing bottle.

"It'll make you sick," he says. His voice is as gentle as if he were touching me. "Warm like that."

But I cannot put the bottle to my mouth. Not where his enormous teeth have been. He is something that has risen out of this day, out of the black and overwhelming power of these towns strung between and under mountains and over mines, a heat-blister out of the day, his green eyes glittering through his hair with the snore of the fan blowing beer fumes over me.

"Did you deliver in Hillcrest?" his soft voice asks.

"Hillcr . . . wha . . . no, no . . . no."

"You wouldn't. Not today, that's when it happened, June 19, 1914. Forty years, today."

His hands clutch the top cases and I cannot move. He is so close the dirt stands grained and polished in his skin bit by bit.

"A tiny fire jumped up, poof! In those miles of tunnels crossing each other two thousand feet inside Hillcrest Mountain, and then the fire licked along the methane gas bleeding along the tops of the tunnels and found the coal dust, here, there, the pockets where the miners were working and it exploded . . . wauggghhh! . . . and the ventilator shafts blew out and then all the oxygen left in the tunnels burned, bright blue like thunder and lightning breaking, and all the miners . . ." his face, hands, body are changing like a rubber horror-mask, bursting from one contortion into another, his body curling up, jerking open spastically . . . "they breathe fire . . . the last oxygen burning, explosion after explosion . . . in the darkness inside the mountain they begin to come apart."

Gradually his face hardens again, his arms, head, shoulders are all there, together.

"Only their brass identification tags gleam in the stinking smoke when the rescue lamps . . . Hillcrest Collieries Limited, June 19, 1914. One hundred eighty-nine men. From Peter Ackers to Michael Zaska."

The coated bottle still sticks in my hand. The truck is twenty cases long: each narrow body is a row of cases, to lay them tight side by side will take nine . . . nine and a half. . . .

"That was my shift," his soft voice goes on, "I was called, yes, I was called but my leg ached. So my friend took my shift. There was never a body found with his brass tag on it. His unchangeable number. We found, we assembled one hundred eighty-eight bodies, and then we had one leg left over."

The sun winks between the four chimneys, the immense crossed tipple of Coleman Collieries. A tiny smoke forms there, disappears grey into the brilliant sky.

"Forty years ago, today," the old man says. "Listen, I have to tell you their names. Listen, there was Ackers, Peter. Adlam, Herbert. Albanese, Dominic. Albanese, Nicholas. Anderson. . . ."

I have to run, run! But he is below me, between me and the door I must reach so I scramble, clanking over the empties and scrape my leg along a case wire but I am down, somehow half-falling and look under the truck—will he move, will he?—and I see one leg there, motionless, beside the tire and then his hair, his head lowers, upside down, it looks like nothing human and at the top of it the terrible mouth is opening on another name and it reaches out for me like a long black tunnel, O sweetest, sweetest Jesus. . . .

"I have only one leg," it whispers, "I have only one. . . ."

The truck spins past me, his head coming up—"Androski, Geor"—and the door under the beer-scummed fan, and darkness. Like a moist hand clapping shut over me. . . but it is open too, and high everywhere, I reach out my arms and there is nothing. Only this moist, slipping, darkness.

"Daddy. . . ."

But there is a light, behind a high narrow table and a shadow moves there, light and glass, misshapen bottles everywhere. And there are other shadows too: quick little double movements of light that come and go, and then I know suddenly those are the eyes. Turned to me from the vastness of the cavern which I cannot see the end of, that is breathing around me like an animal opening itself endlessly for me into close, moist terror—

"DADDY!"

"Del," a huge voice from the light and as my heart jerks I feel my father's hands on my shoulders, his big hands hold me as only they can. They lift me, completely, and his chest, his neck is there too. His gentle breath.

"...Prosper. Davidson, John. Demchuk, George," murmers the mound between wall and telephone post. My father places two warm bottles of Coca-Cola beside it. "Demchuk, Nicholas. Dickenson, Matth...."

The Crowsnest River burbles between boulders around a small island and then bends, vanishes over Lundbreck Falls in quick, slipping silence. In the water I can see that the western sky between the Crowsnest mountains is covered with giant flames. They do not vanish but grow motionlessly larger, upward from the limits of the world and if it were not for the deep sound of water below, I know I could hear the sky burning there.

"The mines are finished," my father says. "Everything's oil and gas now, coal is nothing."

We move slowly east toward the flat darkness. I curl up on the seat, my head in the bend of his thigh. I can hear his muscles shift against my ear as he controls the pedals, the levers, and when we are level at last and up to speed his right hand comes to rest heavy and cupped on my hip. But behind my eyelids I am not asleep; in fact, I may never be able to sleep again.

Queen Elizabeth and Prince Philip visit Chipman as part of
their 1978 tour of the province.

Albertans prepare to honour their queen.

With the Commonwealth Games and a royal visit, it was a
summer to remember.

Opening ceremonies, XI Commonwealth Games, Edmonton.

Celebrations surrounding the Games. An entire city takes part.

The raft race is a highlight of the annual Klondike Days in Edmonton.

Sunday afternoon on the first tee, ninth and eighteenth greens,
Victoria Golf Links, Edmonton.

Big Chief Mountain looms over a hay barn near Police Outpost
Provincial Park.

The prairie at its loneliest, near Finnegan, southern Alberta.

Milk River RCMP post at Writing-on-Stone
Provincial Park.

Upper: Mushroom at Celestine Lake.

Lower: The wild rose, Alberta's provincial flower.

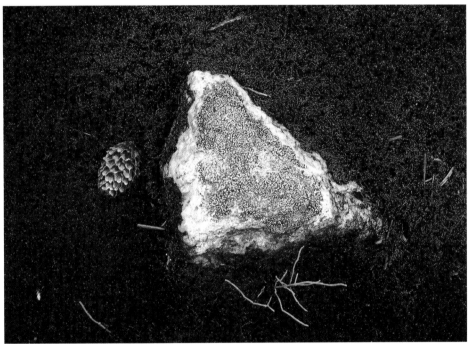

Upper: Western wood lilies near Gold Creek cemetery.

Lower: Pine cone and moss at Waterton Lakes National Park.

Wilhelm Magnussen Raade, 82-year-old outdoorsman and
painter, Calgary.

The gentle beginnings of the Porcupine Hills, west of
Claresholm.

These hoodoos near East Coulee lie in the badlands carved by the Red Deer River. It is through these eerie valleys that paleontologists have wandered for most of this century, looking for evidence of dinosaurs.

Graveyard near Willingdon. The town itself was once called
Agricola, but its name was changed to honour Lord
Willingdon, Governor General of Canada 1926-31.

Abandoned one-room schoolhouse near the hamlet of Aetna,
an early Mormon community.

Bears, All the Time Bears

Why is it, all summer all you hear in the mountain parks is bear stories? I mean "stories" as in "jokes," so-called. Like the old klunker a otherwise pretty guide told us on the Maligne Lake boat cruise: How do you stop a bear from charging? Answer: Take away his credit card. And she expected us to laugh. Some idiots did.

You see more deer than bear in parks, but nobody tells stories that are supposed to be funny about them. Nor mountain sheep. They're pathetic, mooching along the highways all summer and nibbling junk from some kid's hand while mama shrieks, "Be careful—O—they're so cute!" and papa squeezes off another fifty feet of 8 mm. and then in fall with their digestion wrecked and the tourists gone, either the long-distance truckers wheeling through smash them or they go belly-up because there's no barbecued potato chips growing in the grass. I mean, I take pictures too, sure, but any junk food I buy my kids eat; their stomachs can take it.

My son—I only have one, also four girls, all older—my son Havre and I took that Athabasca River Raft Ride and there we heard the silliest bear story of all. You'd figure that for a two-hour ride at $12.75 per adult and $6.50 under twelve—since when is a thirteen-year-old adult?—they'd have quality stories when there's nothing but the usual scenery sliding past, which is most of the time with Edith Cavell sharp and frozen enough but looking more or less always the same in the background. Our raftsman with muscles like Pete Rose handles the raft's big sweep easy as a toothpick through rapids and you figure in the calm he'll come up with a man's story, but he pulls one out about a guide, four nuns, and a grizzly! They meet this big grizzly on a mountain path and the guide tells the nuns just keep calm and take one step back. They do, and the grizzly takes one step forward. The guide tells them just keep calm and take two steps back. They do, and the grizzly takes two steps forward. The nuns don't think too much of their guide's advice about then so they try their own technique: they kneel down and start to pray. And sure enough, the grizzly kneels down and folds his paws just like he's praying too and the nuns get real happy, see, he's religious, he won't bother us. "Nah," the guide says all grey and shaking, "he's the worst kind. He's just saying grace."

Some clods practically fall in the river laughing at that one. I had to give little Havre a bat, he was laughing too. We ran through the long rapids then just opposite Belchers Cabins and for a while that kept me busy hanging on with Havre yelling like a Red Indian and all the women aboard—I had sent my wife and the girls to take some good pictures of flowers—shrieking, grabbing their men like they wanted to throttle them right there in their own life jackets, but then I got to thinking: would that story have such a kick had it been a bull moose? No. And just tourists, not nuns? No again. The joke is in the danger: like this raft ride, you want to be scared but you want to know for sure it isn't really deadly—they tell you three times when you buy the raft ticket they've never lost a passenger yet, not even bust a neck—just the *feeling* of danger maybe. That's it, that *and* the religion: danger and making fun of religion, there you've got the biggest laugh multipliers of all. Kneel down to pray and nowadays somebody will kill himself laughing.

The wife says there are worse ways of going. That night a bear—no grizzly, just ordinary black but big enough that's for sure—a bear comes out of the bush by our campsite. I like to get close to nature and they give us a site—they've got over seven hundred of them, all full all summer—on the outer edge, right up against Whistler Mountain. So of course where does this bear come first?

One of my girls screams and two others drop their wieners into the fire and my wife says, "Into the truck, quick!" and shoos all five kids in the back there where we all sleep, but the bear doesn't come to us: he goes next door, number 29-A, where they've got a nice blue tent beside a table piled up with utensils and they've gone to see the nature film at the amphitheatre. That's the modern way, nature only happens on films. Anyway, it's 10:45 and this bear starts a rumble on that table and campers come running, gawking, and some idiot is taking flash pictures at sixty feet and I'm yelling at this bear to stop busting good equipment, waving my yellow plastic waterpail but he doesn't even bother to give me a side-glance until he's knocked everything over and it's clear there's nothing to eat there and without looking up he comes toward us, number 29-B, in that slope-shouldered easy sideways four-wheel-drive motion they have, ha! The wife and I are around the corner of the truck and the campers are screaming at their kids to get back and I peek around the corner and holy maloney there sits our silver 7-Up cooler! On the table, stuffed full of our breakfast. This flashes through my head and the bear is still coming—the campsites really are nicely spaced—and all of a sudden there's Havre out of the truck heading for the cooler too! Thank god the bear beats him to it. Havre's yelling and waving his arms like he was shooing a chicken and I've got him by the seat of the pants and throw him behind me and the wife catches him before his head bounces off the truck bumper and then that bear looks me in the eye: his two front paws are up on the cooler but it's good stuff, it doesn't open or bend and when I throw the water from my pail at him his head swings up and he looks at me and I know he'll charge, never mind the credit cards, and I try to scramble back, scrunch, and of course I fall flat on my can.

You know that old one about your whole life flashing by before your eyes? Forget it. When you look into the little close-together eyes of a black bear swinging his head around mad, your ticker stops dead and there's nothing but simple flush-everything-out-in-one-woosh terror. I'm on my back, my wife is grabbing for my arm and screaming, Havre is grabbing and screaming, the girls are all screaming in different keys and I'm trying to move and I don't know if I'm still alive and I *am* still alive because that bear has not charged!

The screams don't matter to him. He has knocked that 7-Up cooler off the table and is rolling it backward under the trees, end over end, and walking backward like a circus dog doing tricks and finally the lid pops off and he stops, fifty feet away, to have a look. Four pounds of hamburger, two of bacon, a dozen eggs, two loaves of bread, butter, four quarts of milk, mayonnaise: could be worse. He settles down right there and has a picnic. Half an hour; nobody, but nobody bothers him.

Eleven-fifteen; out on the prairie it would still be light but against the mountain we can barely see him, nothing but a dark blotch when he pushes the cooler away, stands up and swings his head around, then continues on to 29-C, 29-D, perfectly alphabetical. But everybody's stowed everything in their vehicles and he's sniffing around 29-M when the ranger finally gets there and throws a firecracker at him that explodes like a cannon and he, without any rush but like that were some sort of signal, lopes off sideways into the dark. He'll be back now, the ranger says looking at me sour as pickles, tomorrow for sure and they'll have to try and shoot him with a tranquillizer and haul him way back into the mountains.

So I got dirty looks besides all the embarrassment. When our neighbours got back from their nice nature film about twenty people told them why their equipment was so messed up and then they all looked at me trying to bend my cooler straight—all that was left in it was the jar of mayonnaise, open but uneaten—and sort of chuckled. We pulled out for the Columbia Icefields real early next morning. And I'll tell you one thing. If I ever hear some guide tell a story about some hell-fire preacher in a big Winnebago trying to shoo away a bear rattling empty cans at his neighbour's while he's got a full hamper of food standing right beside him, I won't be held responsible for what happens.

After Thirty Years of Marriage

After thirty years of marriage and six children, Papa and my total worldly wealth was a mortgaged house in Rockford, Illinois, and a plot in the Rockford cemetery where little John Wesley had been lying for sixteen years. Land in Illinois cost a hundred dollars an acre; we cleared a thousand dollars from the sale of our house and on March 20, 1906, Papa and our second youngest son, Jolson, boarded the train for Red Deer, Alberta. With three men over eighteen left in the family, we could file on 480 acres of free land; a few years of hard work on that much land and we believed we would return to the States with enough money so our three youngest sons Ethan, Jolson and Billings (still too young to file, unfortunately) could go to school and Papa and me retire in some comfort.

There was, of course, no land available near Red Deer. Actually, of the thirty-six sections in any Alberta township, sixteen are already owned by the CPR, one by the Hudson's Bay Company, and two reserved for schools, so that only seventeen widely scattered sections, the even-numbered ones, can ever be homesteaded on. When Ethan and Billings and I arrived in Alberta near the end of June, we travelled to the railhead which was then at Stettler. There we found Papa and Jolson shingling, their lips purple with nails, and after many colourful kisses they told us they had filed sight-unseen on land seventy miles east and our first problem would be to get there. I had a migraine headache from sitting up four days and nights on trains but I managed to cook my first Canadian meal to hugged and kissed acclaim.

I had been able to borrow an extra two hundred dollars in Illinois. That was not nearly enough for a team of horses, but together with what Papa and Jolson had earned building in Stettler, we purchased two oxen. One was a blotchy red, the other coal black, and both had great extended ears that waved in time with their majestic pace. They were immediately christened Tom and Bruce, good short names for yelling, Papa said, and when we harnessed them, put bits in their mouths, and hitched them to the wagon, we found them as fundamentally opposed to motion as any mountain, but ever faithful and above all patient. That compensated for almost everything. How often I leaned against Tom's powerful shoulder and cried until I had no tears left, and he would turn his flat, triangular head toward me, his eyes so steady and unchanging. We had them both as long as we were in Alberta.

Papa and Jolson had taken a hunting knife and shotgun with them, and Ethan (not to be outdone) bought a .30-30 for eighteen dollars. It seemed a very large amount of money to me, but it proved its value the second day out from Stettler. There were ducks on the sloughs (as they call the ponds here) everywhere, but far too wary for a shotgun so when we saw a lovely goose stretching its neck at us out of the bulrushes, Ethan got out his big gun. Papa laughed, "You'll blow it to pieces!" And sure enough, when Ethan leaned on the wagon and fired, the goose vanished as the ducks rose in a frightful clatter. Billings waded out and discovered the bullet had slit its jugular vein! Ethan never fired that gun again—we never saw an animal around the homestead that needed it—so his marksmanship became a family legend, and though the goose was excellent, I always thought it too dear at eighteen dollars plus a bullet. Later that summer Jolson stacked hay; by saving every single penny, he brought home twenty dollars for a month's work.

When we found the iron peg with four square holes dug around it that marked the corner of one of our quarter sections, we all went a little daffy. We had been travelling for five days at ox-pace over open land the colour of burnt bread, land which none of us could have ever imagined. We would see a settler's sod house or board shanty four hours before we passed it, and at most we saw three a day. Papa jumped from the wagon, "I want to enter first," and Ethan said, "I'm with you," and then all three boys had jumped off, even young

Billings, and with their hands on Papa's shoulders they walked onto the promised land together while I watched them over the backs of the oxen. Then we oriented ourselves to the sun and by the end of the day had found our other two quarters. There was one homesteader near us, three miles southwest, and Ethan got a pail of water from his barrel and with the wood we had carried with us we made camp. That Mr. Williams, who had been a Union soldier during the Civil War, brought us luck: when Papa and the boys began digging a well beside our tent the next morning, they struck cold fresh water nine feet down; the land looked so featureless, slightly rolling and covered with buffalo grass, that the only reason we camped there was because I felt I had to be in sight of the Williams's cabin.

Though it was barely July, all the things that had to be done before winter almost made us dizzy, just to list them. When our eyes grew accustomed to distance, we discovered other homesteaders about us: almost all of them from the States, but no one had time for a July 4 celebration that year. We had a well, a very great blessing, but we had to buy a cow and chickens, fence, put up hay, and above all build a house and barns for ourselves and our animals. Besides that, we had to find wood to burn and also break land so that next spring we could seed and grow our first cash crop. In the meantime, we had to live on our resources, such as they were, and so instead of all the boys being able to help Papa steadily, both Ethan and Jolson hired out to neighbouring ranchers and settlers for fencing, haying, any kind of heavy work that could be got. We needed the cash to buy food and clothing for the hard winter that everyone who had lived in the country for a year took great joy in assuring us was certainly ahead. If I had known then that the winter of 1906-7 would be the worst in the living memory of anyone on the Canadian prairies, I know I would have despaired. But I did not know, and I suppose that was for the better.

Actually, the summer was very pleasant, and at first I was not really afraid of the endless space all around. The mosquitoes were more or less over after about two weeks, though not completely gone till September, and Papa discovered that there were wooded hills southwest of us, enormous numbers of gnarled and dead aspen so we could haul as much firewood as we pleased. I refused to live in a sod shanty; I knew it was cheap and warm but I also knew it was like a tent—quite impossible to keep clean—and though the trees were too short to build a conventional house of horizontal logs, they gave me an idea. I sketched it on the back of a milk-can label and within a week Jolson had dug a trench for the foundation of the house twenty-eight by eighteen feet. Its walls were to be made of two rows of vertical poles with the space between them filled with mud from the lake. There was not another house like it in the entire country, and after we had spent the winter in it we knew why. But it seemed fine at the time, though it required nine loads of logs and forty tons (as the boys estimated) of mud just for the walls. We moved out of the tent into it on Saturday, October 20, 1906. The roof had not been completed and that night I was as cold as I had ever been in my life. The wind howled so dreadfully I did not know how I would have endured it in the tent hammering, jerking on its ropes. That is perhaps the worst of living on the Alberta prairie: the wind. There is not a bush anywhere, and it gets a two-hundred-mile clean run at you from the mountains.

But that was the coming of winter. Summer was beautiful, and I had never seen such skies or light. From the wooded hills the prairie spread east like water falling away, wind brushing the grass and the small sloughs everywhere dark green and blue and indigo and the horizon merging with the sky in a bluish dust. On the CPR section beside us lay the perfect circle of a pond surrounded by willows, the water so sweet it must have been fed by springs, and the paths of the buffalo radiated from it like the spokes of a wheel cut two and three feet into the ground; in the long evenings when the light settled down like a slow blanket, you could so easily imagine those huge black shapes coming single file from all directions towards the last bright centre of water, silent, moving lower and lower into the earth cut by their paths. Then suddenly the ducks would begin talking: gossipy old women among the rushes so loud I could hear them a mile away in the tent complaining, comparing children, and bang! Billings's shotgun would explode, bang again as the ducks splattered up and away, and soon I would be plucking—hopefully mallards because they were the largest and always the fattest for some reason—and at sunset Papa and Ethan and Jolson would have meat to fill their stomachs, empty from all day cutting and stacking hay: they each wanted half a duck at least, or a whole prairie chicken.

The Alberta sunsets were beyond description. Such burning reds I never saw anywhere again, either in nature or art. It seemed to me then that if this world is finally to be judged by fire, surely that fire has been kindled already.

Cooking? How did I cook. Like a squaw at an open fire mostly, bending there until I was more smoked than my meal cooked. I had few enough cooking worries; there came a time when eating potatoes and oatmeal was nearly as monotonous as cooking them. Until our stove arrived from Illinois—in September—I had to walk to Williams's every other day with my dough and an armful of wood to bake four loaves in their stove. Often, on that endless walk with my arms numb with those seemingly light things I was carrying, I found a rock or badger mound to sit on and cry. An especially good place for this was "Buffalo Rock," a huge stone in a hollow worn out by hooves of buffalo itching themselves. I sat there, my head against that rock rubbed smooth as marble, but when Billings came with me, we two swinging the dough pan between us and both of us with half an armful of wood, then we stopped there to rest only, to drink some water and laugh at the gophers chasing each other so easily across the prairie. How handy to live in the ground, he said once, to have a smooth pointed body that could whistle in and out of narrow tunnels. No tent to clutch desperately in wind or thunderstorm, and covered with fur against both flies and mosquitoes.

That was best about outdoor cooking: the soaring pests disliked smoke. Of course we had smudges in the evening, but the tent could not be tied up tight in the hot nights and no one can sleep in a cloud of smoke, so we really had no protection. Sometimes towards evening the oxen were neither red nor black, simply grey with mosquitoes. And the flies, they piled up double on everything. As Papa said one late supper, "It's a great comfort to eat in the dark. You don't know what all you're eating."

Every time I was down with my two- or three-day headaches, I felt these terrible insects would finish me, whining, crawling, burrowing everywhere. Actually there were homesteaders who gave up their claims because of them. Perhaps the women did it. The men had hard daily drudgery to weary them so they slept through insects and storm too; above all, they had the visible results of a house wall or an acre of ploughing to prove themselves, but women have to keep at the same few things over and over and wait for their men to come from wherever they are. I could never see my men haying because, though it appears flat, the prairie is filled with slopes and hollows; wherever I looked there was simply the endless horizon. For days then I saw no living, moving thing from the tent, and I never dared venture from it for fear I would be lost—I never did lose myself, but I always had the numb ache that I would. When I finally saw a distant moving wagon, or a herd of cattle filing at noon toward the sweet pond to drink, I felt a relief, a companionship I rarely knew in Rockford when my neighbours came for afternoon tea.

I have never been one to complain, and I won't begin now, but pioneering is work for very strong people, or a group of people like ourselves who have various strengths between them. Many people came to Alberta not knowing that. For someone alone, or if Papa had had only me, we could not have lasted a month. But our boys were unbelievable; I never knew my oldest three children, grown up and happily married in Illinois, the way I now knew these last three, the way they tackled problems that would have turned an old person grey, worked for months on ranches or on railway crews where gambling and loose living destroyed many married men while our boys brought home every penny they earned, laughing and telling us endless stories. I remember one terrible day when the heat and flies had literally hammered me flat and my migraine had built to such a pressure that I knew the plates of my skull were bouncing, grinding together in agony, and then toward evening I heard Billings come home singing at the top of his voice, "Back, back, back to Baltimore!", his high boyish sound floating as if it came from everywhere around me and I struggled to my feet and came out of the tent and the sun was low and mellow beyond the horizon like a burning town; I just hugged him all sweaty and he gave me a fast squeeze, not seeing my tears. "There are so many flowers," he said, pushing back, "it's too bad we have to tear them up with the plough."

And the people. The best thing about homesteading is that everyone begins at the same place, really with nothing but themselves on the empty land. That's true no matter how many "things" you bring with you: you struggle with the mosquitoes, the water, the wood, the loneliness, the space and distance all around; that is, the land. After a year this begins to change, and by the end of the second summer when the hail had smashed some of our crops into our new ploughing and others got fifty bushels to the acre, the pioneering oneness clearly began to go, go forever. But the first year: I used the Williams's stove, they came to our good well for drinking water; Papa used Erik Olsen's haymower while he ploughed with our plough. If you had something a neighbour needed, or ate a meal when the neighbour came by, you shared. That was the strange, human effect the first year with a new land had on all of us, and for some it was so strong that it did not vanish, Billings told me later, to the ends of their lives.

The prairie fire of May 12, 1907, had the entire country fighting it, together. Though we had seen a few distant fires in the late fall, the worst season is early spring just before the green grass comes. The fire travels on the wind, and with its own terrible heat creates such a draft that often no running horse can stay ahead of it; the only protection is a slough or ploughed land or a backfire—anything which deprives it of fuel—and if these barriers are too narrow the headfire will simply leap over them. That day a father six miles south of us had gone to the timber—why he would leave when the smoke had been visible all day before and the smell of burning on the evening air, I don't know—and left a girl alone with an invalid mother and three little children. The house was poorly fireguarded, and the girl led the children to the ploughed field and told them to sit there together and not move or look anywhere while she went back for the mother. But the children must have been terrified: they started back toward home and so when the father returned home, driving furiously from the hills when he noticed the fire, he found his house and stacks and barns in ashes and himself the only survivor of his entire family.

We saw the high smoke when we got up that morning, and the wind was from the southeast. Ethan rode south (we had a pony by then) to the ridges while Papa and Jolson ploughed a wider fireguard and Billings and I laid out sacks and set pails of water. Soon Ethan returned as fast as his horse could gallop, but by that time we could already see the flames and smoke driving across the hills only three miles away. The men quickly began setting a line of small fires farther and farther south, very carefully: if you set too wide a backfire, you can create a prairie fire of your own. A family north of us started a backfire two miles from their house, just to be sure, and burned down their homestead before the wild fire even reached them. But despite the black wedge of prairie on two sides of us, the approach of that fire was awesome. The men went forward with the neighbours to see if they could turn the headfire; but Billings and I had to stay at the house with sacks and pails: if the fire got past the men and jumped the guard, we would have to scream for help and try to control it until help came.

The fire burns in a wedge. The headfire at its point creates such a flaming whirlwind that it rushes ahead as if it were following a trail of gunpowder. Nothing can stop a headfire in May prairie grass on a windy day. The boys fought toward it with sacks soaked in water, the smoke suffocating, and then suddenly the smoke lifted in the wind and they saw a wall of flames driving toward them and they ran, desperately, and if the freshwater pond had not been within twenty yards of them, they and the horse would have burned alive. Ethan rode, Jolson jumped right into the water, and the flames passed them like a giant locomotive roaring past a station.

"Maybe it caught Papa!" Ethan gasped. "On the other side."

Jolson was already pulling himself out of the muck. "Come on!" he shouted and ran across the smoking grass leaping with scattered patches of fire. Ethan had a longer struggle to get the frightened horse across.

But Papa was all right; he and the neighbours had stopped the western sidefires so when Jolson sprinted up their only concern was us and the homestead. I saw that headfire approaching, and with Billings beside me felt so totally helpless, a puny human nailed to the ground with a wet sack in her hands and that inhuman scourge roaring. . .the backfire and guards made it hesitate, just for an instant, and Billings screamed, "It'll stop, Mama, see, see!", but it would not have, I know, that momentary hesitation was nothing to that horrible furnace driving at us but then like a breath from heaven a westerly crosswind wafted over us, unbelievably, and perhaps all the people in the country were praying with me and Billings and Papa and Ethan and Jolson. For like a startled animal that headfire leaned, suddenly leaped sideways and roared around us along the east side of our guard, northward. When the men ran up, scorched and gasping, Billings and I were slapping out the last bits of flame on the haystack and the house roof. Papa kissed me, right in front of everyone, and then they ran off north and east after the slowly spreading sidefires. The headfire didn't die until it ran into the big lake seven miles north of us.

Such a black smoking world you cannot imagine. We were a grey island in the deepest corner of hell. Wherever you stepped your feet burned, smoke sprang at you. But a day later it rained, a warm, soft, penetrating rain and the glory of grass and flowers that grew out of those ashes within a week I cannot describe. The wonders of the world are endless, how out of the greatest terror God surprises us again and again with more beauty and goodness than we ever had before.

That was our first spring, after we had come through the winter of 1906-7. We had lived it in our unique house, of course, and that was a mixed blessing too. The house was clean enough after the tent: once, during the summer I had gotten out my broom and leaned it against the front of the tent, not with the intention of sweeping anything (after all not even I, as Ethan pointed out, could clean up the whole prairie) but just to remind me of a future hope; however, the house was cold. Indescribably. The wall of lake-mud dried, cracked, and we could not fill the cracks carefully enough. I put on my heaviest clothes for bed, and in the morning granules of snow were sifted over me, my breath frozen into ice on my pillow. I have never been so cold, and during my headaches the house became worse than Hades. The men could not, of course, stay all day with me during my sickness, not even Billings because there was so much work to do and I did not want them to stay: I preferred my agony alone, to their restless impatience, but how often I prayed for the understanding hand of a woman. Very few homesteaders wintered on their claims; they returned East or moved into town, but since so much of our summer energy had gone into building the disastrous house at my insistence, we could not afford that. However, one of our absent neighbours had a little organ which they permitted us to use for the winter, and I do believe it saved my sanity. I would play, pumping furiously, singing every song I knew and pieces I made up so loudly that Ethan swore he heard it all the way to Mr. Mason's store and post office, three miles above the howling wind. I told him he'd freeze his ears if he didn't keep them covered.

But one day in February not even the organ helped. Both Ethan and Jolson were working away at the time and Papa and Billings had been fixing the barn against the hard storms; I was the second day into a migraine and about three o'clock Papa said he should go to Mason's as there had been no blizzard and probably the mail had come in. Billings looked at me so longingly that I said he should go along, but please, come home quickly. So they trudged off into the snow, and I waited.

Five hours! I made supper for six o'clock, as usual, but nothing. I wanted to rush out, search, but of course there were two of them and besides I was terrified of the winter prairie. My head hammered; my feet were blue with cold no matter how much wood I banged into the

174

stove. And outside lay that vast motionless stillness which comes only before the worst storms, a night where the moonlight turns the endless waves of snow into rigid, frozen steel. And when those two men finally came in, with no mail, they said they'd been choring in the barn for half an hour, just so they could save putting on their mackinaws again and oh they were sorry they hadn't bothered to tell me they were back!

I got out of bed, thrust my feet into my old slippers, and started for the door in my nightgown.

"Sara," Papa said, "where are you going?"

"Outside. To stand on my head in a snowdrift."

Papa and Billings sank back into their chairs, their arms hanging down limp, the most marvellous expression of helplessness on their faces.

"Why Sar," Papa said finally, "I believe you're crazy."

"I *know* it," and I got the door wrenched open and marched around to the west side of the house where the drifts were the deepest. I broke the crust, knelt down and stuck my head into the snow as deeply as I could without smothering and I held it there until it felt quite frozen and all the rest of me too. Then I picked up a big piece of snow and went back into the house. The men sat there, looking at me, not having moved a muscle. I wrapped the snow in a towel and lay down on it like a pillow and I slept without waking or dream and in the morning my headache had vanished and so had my temper.

We stayed five years in Alberta, and we stayed that long because of Billings. Our first crop was smashed by hail so we couldn't sell out or leave that year, but then the crops were steadily better as we ploughed more land and also bought cattle so that in three years Ethan could enrol in the winter session at the University of Chicago and Jolson was taking correspondence courses from there too. They both studied until they finished their PH.D.'s and became professors, thanks to our Alberta homestead, but Billings returned to Alberta after a year of high school in Illinois and he refused to go back. We could not talk him out of it. So we stayed for five years: he was nineteen then and he bought Ethan's and Jolson's quarters with money he borrowed against our quarter, which we gave him outright, and he stayed on to become one of the genuine old-timers of the district. He even became a Canadian citizen and celebrated the first of July instead of the fourth. Papa and I returned to Illinois, more bent perhaps and certainly no richer, but we had been able to give our last three sons the start they wanted in life, though one was very different from the way we had foreseen it.

Best of all, however, were those years together. How we loved and cared for each other as we worked side by side on our Alberta homestead, sharing hardship and triumph, joy and sorrow. Not many parents have such a memory.

Edward Cardinal, ninety-six years old, poses with his
great-grandchildren on the Saddle Lake Reserve.

Looking east along Highway 500 toward Writing-on-Stone
Provincial Park. The park has many remarkable examples of
ancient Indian picture writing inscribed on the sandstone cliffs
of the Milk River valley.

A Cree dancer.

Joe Large, top marksman, on the Saddle Lake Reserve.

From the summit of the Wintering Hills in early spring one feels
that one can see forever.

Above: Calgary Stampede parade, 1978. The streets through which these Blackfoot chiefs ride have undergone a near-miraculous transformation. It is hard to believe the city of Calgary is less than ninety years old.

Opposite: Toronto Dominion Tower, Calgary. Where not so long ago cowboys ambled down the sunlit streets of a dusty cowtown, pedestrians now stream through and around the soaring towers of one of the fastest-growing financial centres in the western world.

View from Marten Mountain,
Lesser Slave Lake.

Children's day is always a highlight of the Saddle Lake
pow-wow, an annual event well known throughout
northeastern Alberta.

Winnie and Thomas Wasateneau of Saddle Lake are a
traditional couple who still get their water from a well and their
heat from a wood-burning stove.

Chicken dance.

The tribe gathers for the annual Indian Days festivities.

Indian children, Saddle Lake Reserve.

Upper: Paint peels from the wall of an old building on
the reserve.

Lower: A new generation of Native people will play an
important part in Alberta's future.

Foxgrass near Little Fish Lake.

Seen here one year before his death at the age of ninety-two,
Ben Moses had just walked four miles from his snares in the
back country of northeastern Alberta.

Mrs. Louise Cardinal.

From Montreal, 1848

My family emigrated from Berwick-on-Tweed, Scotland, in 1832, and I was born in Montreal on December 20 of the same year. On March 3, 1848, I bound myself to the service of the Hudson's Bay Company for five years at ten pounds a year and in early April we left Lachine in three Rice canoes, eighteen paddles to each canoe, for the wild, unknown West. I was fifteen, and my contract had mentioned nothing about bedding so the first night I spent blanketless before the fire and cried out my homesickness.

Next morning I felt much better and bought two blankets from a trader. We paddled via Bytown (now Ottawa), Lake Huron, Fort William, Rat Portage and Norway House to York Factory on Hudson Bay where we met the Saskatchewan Brigade on July 10. From there we paddled and tracked with the brigade (thirteen canoes of eight men each led by Chief Factor Rowand, an incarnate fiend who would curse you blind if you looked sideways) back to Norway House, across Lake Winnipeg and up the Saskatchewan River past Forts Carlton and Pitt to Edmonton. When we arrived there on September 26, I discovered I had been assigned to Rocky Mountain House, 250 miles upriver. I was given a horse (I had never been on one before) that looked like a box of cutlery and told, "Ride." We finally reached our winter quarters on November 2.

That endless season was the worst part of my life, so far. I had two quarrels with fellow greenhorns; both times the brigade boss ordered us to fight it out and both times I was pounded flat and kicked purple. Life was all work, eat and sleep. The sleep was merciful oblivion, the work of paddling, tracking and portaging was labour (not much), drudgery (more), and exhaustion (mostly). I do not remember seeing anything, what I remember is food.

We began at Lachine with the old staples of pork and peas and black quarter-pound biscuits. When we wanted coffee, we burnt the biscuits and added water. But our real drink was three drams of rum per day, strong and warm in your gut. When we reached Sault Ste. Marie we recruits were locked in a warehouse for fear we would "skip" to the American side; we discovered a sack of raisins in a corner and ate so much that during the night our grandmothers came and made faces at us. After that we got nothing but corn, greased with tallow to make it slide down, till we reached Rainy River and saw our first pemmican. We crowded around a hundred-pound hide sack (hair outside) and nibbled a sample. My first mouthful made me sick, but I got over that. We made rab-a-bo, pemmican mixed with a little flour and boiled in water. When cooked it looked something like soup and could be eaten either with spoon or knife, and since our rum ration had been stopped long ago, we had nothing to help it down. We ate that for forty-one days to York Factory where we each received a loaf of bread, two pounds of pork and a whole quart of rum! You can understand why all the brigade men were big powerful men: weak chaps got killed off.

For two days out of York (beginning July 24) we ate "regal," then we were back to rab-a-bo. We called it a-bo-rab and bo-rab-a but it tasted more or less the same, so we dreamt of buffalo. We were tracking now (that is, pulling loaded York boats upriver with ropes) and at The Pas we laid in a welcome stock of potatoes. Finally, on August 31 at Wives Hill near Carlton, the Crees appeared with fresh buffalo meat. Every manjack of us ate until he could hold no more, and a good number were seasick among the dry bushes for it. Then all the way to Edmonton, tracking four hours on, four hours off, from morning till night, we had twenty-seven days of uninterrupted buffalo. Edmonton itself was flour, pemmican and buffalo, so our first camp out of Edmonton, at White Mud Creek on October 9, we killed seventy-five rabbits and stuffed ourselves. Then we had nothing but rabbits until we reached winter quarters November 2.

Work, sleep, and eat: that was my first Rocky Mountain winter. Evenings were endless and I had nothing to read: I did not get my first mail (three letters from my mother and two copies of the Montreal *Witness*) until a year later, September 1849. By that time, however, I had won my first fight and begun visiting the women. Being young and quick to learn, I soon spoke as much Cree as was necessary.

The Year We Gave Away the Land

I remember each year of my long life as easily as I finger a string of beads; each bead is one particular thing that happened. But no Blackfoot can forget the year the whites count 1877. That was the year we gave away the land. I will tell you how it was.

Sunday, September 16

The Queen's white commissioner came with eighty Mounted Police and forty wagons over the round hills of the Bow River at the Crossing. Up on the prairie we had seen their dust curl all day, but still their white helmets and red coats shone in the sun, a long stiff worm of red and white and gleaming horses coming down into the valley with a white-fisted drummer rattling them ahead as they rode. Two of the wagons had those guns so big you can stick your fist into the barrels.

But at Blackfoot Crossing there were only Old Sun's and Crowfoot's bands of the Siksikas to watch them, and the Stoneys camped across the river running together to stare. Not a single Piegan or Sarcee had come, and I and my forty young men were the only Bloods. Without women or children, we could have been on a raid. We sat on our horses, watching. They came across the river flat, straight like whites do everything, straight, one wagon with a square canvas to keep the sun off the commissioner's blotchy face. They came bumping under the flags, straight to where the trees open on the Crossing. There Colonel Macleod lifted his hand and everything stopped. The police swung down and after a minute the blotchy man unbent himself, long and bony, out of his wagon.

"Tall Man," someone behind me named him.

And we laughed a little. I had a better name for him later, though I never said it; he was too strong for me. But he did not seem so then, just long and thin, and we stopped watching him because there were more police on the south hills. They were trying to chase grey cattle into the valley.

"There come the presents," someone said, and some of us laughed.

Monday, September 17

A little after noon they fired the guns. The sound rumbled down the valley and sent children and dogs running for shelter. Then all the chiefs went to see Macleod and Tall Man under the canvas inside the squares of police tents, Bear's Paw and his Stoney councillors riding their best horses through the river. But no more people had come in. Old Sun would not open his mouth and Crowfoot said they would have to wait two days, maybe four. Macleod said to me,

"Medicine Calf, do you think Red Crow and Rainy Chief will be here with your people in two days?"

For a minute I looked at Jerry Potts, the guide and interpreter. His mother was a Blood killed in a whisky brawl long before the police came and stopped that; he got paid well by Macleod, and when they had it quite a lot of confiscated whisky too, though he always wanted more.

"Why doesn't he ask Crowfoot again?" I said.

Potts swore, carefully under his hand. "He never understands, he still thinks the Blackfoot Nation has one big head chief."

"That one," I nodded at Crowfoot, "doesn't mind pretending we do." Though if we had, it would have been my chief, Red Crow of the South Bloods. But Red Crow never wanted to talk to whites, so how could they know him?

"What does he say?" Macleod asked Potts.

"He doesn't know," Potts said.

Tall Man was talking. The Mounted Police would give us food, the things piled inside the square and the bony cattle if we needed them, and Bear's Paw stood up and said he wanted everything, yes. But Crowfoot was studying Tall Man, whom none of us had ever seen before.

"We still have buffalo," was all Crowfoot said. And his tone meant what Big Bear had said three years before about treaties: "When we set a fox trap, we scatter meat all around, but when the fox is in the trap we knock him on the head. We want no bait, let your chiefs come like men and talk to us." I fought Big Bear four times. He was a Cree, our enemy, but that time he spoke true.

Macleod and Tall Man looked at each other when Potts translated Crowfoot's four words; they understood meanings. Then Old Sun stood up, and every Blackfoot stood up with him.

Tuesday, September 18
We rode east before dawn along the prairie above the river, and there we ran buffalo as the sun came up blood red. O Great Spirit, the land and the sky! When we returned dragging our travois heavy with meat, Sitting on an Eagle Tail with all his Piegans was at the Crossing, about nine hundred of them. And so were the traders from Fort Macleod and Edmonton, chopping down trees for walls to protect their goods. Many were Montana men. They carried their Winchesters naked on the saddle across their knees. We surrounded them, all bloody from hunting, and told them no treaty had been made and they would not chop down one more tree at this sacred place. So they went to the Mounted Police and Macleod said we were right. While we sat on our horses watching them they stacked their goods back inside their tents.

We danced and ate meat all night with the Piegans. Eiyannah, the stories and the singing!

Wednesday, September 19
When we came to the tent inside the police square the whites were already there, including six white women, more than any of us had ever seen. After the long, hot summer their faces were still like snow under their wide hats, their bright dresses pulled in so tight around the tops of their bodies. My young men stared and stared, such dry women looking shamelessly back at us, but laughing and whispering to each other like Blackfeet.

We chiefs sat down in a half-circle in front of Tall Man and
Macleod, and behind us our prairie people gathered, several thousand
now though Red Crow and the Bloods had not come. Tall Man began
in a high sing-song, and after a moment he stopped, waited. But Jerry
Potts could say nothing. Such speech was impossible for him, he never
translated more than five words, no matter how long the original
statement. Finally an old white man who had lived with the Piegans
for years, he was called Bird, stepped forward. He could talk like a
medicine man and Tall Man started again.

"The Great Spirit has made all things, it is by that Spirit that the
Queen rules over this great country. She loves all her children, both
white and red alike, but she hates wickedness. And that is why she
sent the police to punish the bad men who robbed you with whisky."

"Did your father ever tell you a woman had our country?" Eagle
Ribs asked me. He was war leader of the Siksikas as I was of the
Bloods; we would have to explain all this to our warriors.

On his left Eagle Calf, leader of the Many Children band, said,
"The whites are coming anyway, like in Montana. We should at least
get some of those presents for our land."

"Twenty years ago," I told them, "I signed the Blood treaty with
the Americans in Montana. And now you can't ride anywhere there
without a white watching you. Treaties mean nothing."

"But look, this is Macleod," Eagle Calf said. "He talks for the
Great Mother, he's different."

"He's just white too," Eagle Ribs said staring at the pale smiling
women, their hands folded in their flowered laps.

"Last year," Tall Man was saying, "we made treaty with the Crees,
and now we come to make treaty with the Blackfeet. In a few years the
buffalo will all be destroyed and for this reason the Queen wishes you
to live in some other way. She wishes you to allow her white children
to come and live on your land, raise cattle, grow grain, and she will
assist you to do the same."

"There are so many whites along the Old Man's River already,"
Eagle Ribs said, "they have ruined the hunting."

"She will also pay you," Tall Man shouted, "money every year, money as a gift so you cannot be cheated. Twenty-five dollars for each chief, twelve dollars each for signing, and five dollars every year after that, forever."

"How can we give away land?" Eagle Ribs muttered.

"Maybe we can't give it," Eagle Calf said, "but those whites can sure take it. We better take their presents."

Eagle Ribs was looking at me. "What is that 'money'?"

"Sometimes it's metal, sometimes a piece of paper with a picture. If you have enough of it, sometimes the traders give you a gun."

"Or a dipperful of whisky," Eagle Calf laughed.

"If you sign the treaty," Tall Man shouted, "a reserve of land will be set aside for you and your children forever, for every five persons you will have one square mile of land set aside. Cattle will be given to you, and potatoes like those grown at Fort Macleod. And we will send teachers so your children will learn to read books like this one...."

Tall Man was holding up a black missionary book, and Macleod just sat, nodding his heavy head. But I was hearing the mutter of young men behind me. That blotchy man had said that soon the buffalo would be destroyed. There were so few left now, and the Crees from the north and Sioux from the south were hunting those few also, I knew he was right. Eagle Ribs beside me was thinking my thoughts: the land and the buffalo, how else can prairie people live?

That evening I rode up to the prairie. Bull Head and the Sarcees had come in, they were raising their lodges in the circles of the valley. But Red Crow and Rainy Chief, my wives and children with them, had not come. The sun was gone behind the white teeth of the mountains, and a wind—as if the earth were breathing...hissss uhhh...hisssss uhhh—cold and hard, I could smell winter, I could smell dying. Like the terrible year of the Rotting Sickness when we scraped ourselves bloody against the traders' gateposts, trying to rub off the disease that killed us piece by piece, to give it back to the whites who gave it to us but themselves never suffered from it. The moon bulged up, white and blotchy, out of the land. Who had ever asked for them to come, if we could just kill them all, who would not pray a lifetime if only they could be wiped away like dirt in a sweatlodge?

My horse grazed a little in the dry circle of my reins. The earth under me was hard, warm; it moved so certainly with my breathing. But the police had stopped the whisky trading, the terrible drunkenness that killed us as surely as disease. And now Macleod said, "Sign." Great Spirit, how will we live? How can we live with them?

When the moon was down, I stood up. And prayed. After a time it came to me that war, raid, and defence, which were my life with my people, these were not enough. Words had to be made here. And then Pemmican came to me in my prayer, the old medicine man of my people.

"The buffalo make you strong," were his words. "But what you eat from this money will bury our people all over the hills. You will be tied down, whites will take your land and fill it."

When I opened my eyes, I saw that the long light that comes before dawn had spread my shadow wide, grey across the prairie. A thin grey stick pointing west.

Thursday, September 20
After the guns fired, Crowfoot and Old Sun and Sitting on an Eagle Tail and Bull Head all said they would speak tomorrow. Then I stood up.

"My chief, Red Crow, is not here, but it is time now for defence so I will speak. The Great Spirit, not the Queen, gave us this land. The Queen sent Macleod with the police to stop the whisky. At that time I could not sleep, any sound might be my drunken brother coming to kill me or my children in his drunkenness. Now I can sleep, without being afraid. But there is still the land."

While Bird translated, Crowfoot watched me with his hard, beaked face. He understood whites better than anyone, he had thought about them for years.

"The Great Spirit"—I said loudly, but really to Crowfoot—"it is hard to understand, but He must have sent the whites here to do what

He wants. We Bloods signed a treaty with the Americans twenty years ago, and the first year they gave us large bags of flour and many blankets, the second year only half as much, and now it is nothing but a handful of flour and a rag. The Queen must give us fifty dollars for each chief, thirty dollars for every man, woman, and child. Every year. We must be paid for all the trees the police and the whites have already cut, for there will soon be no firewood left for us. The land . . . the land is too much to give away for so little."

And Tall Man was laughing. "If our police have driven away the whisky traders," he said, "surely you cannot expect us to pay for the timber they used. For helping you so much, by rights you should pay us!"

And I burst out laughing, and all our people with me. Tall Man and Macleod and the police laughed too; but for a different reason, I think.

Crowfoot, however, did not laugh. And that night Red Crow and Rainy Chief with almost two thousand Bloods rode in. The whole valley was now filled with lodges, with the laughter of people and the running of horses. That was the last free gathering of the Blackfoot Nation for though we talked all night in Crowfoot's lodge, though I said again and again that the treaty was too little, and though the North Piegans and Eagle Ribs wanted to wipe out every policeman and the commissioner at dawn and then ride east to the buffalo, nevertheless Red Crow stated he would agree with Crowfoot. And Crowfoot said, "The whites are coming. The Americans make treaties and then their army kills people like rabbits. Macleod treats every white and every Indian exactly the same. What can we do? We have to trust Macleod."

I walked to my lodge and saw the gentle faces of my wives and children. But I did not sleep. At dawn Pemmican came to me again. "The whites will lead you by a halter," he said. "That is why I say, don't sign. But my life is old, over. Sign if you want to. Sign." I could hardly hear his voice, it was so old and broken.

Friday, September 21

All the tribes of the Blackfoot Nation, Siksika, Blood, and Piegan, and our allies the Sarcee, gathered with the Stoneys at the Crossing. And Crowfoot made the long speech the Queen's commissioners had sat up stiff all week to hear.

"Take pity on us with regard to our country, the prairies, the forests and the waters, the animals that live in them. Do not take them from us forever. We are the children of the plains, and the buffalo have been our food always. I hope you look upon the Blackfeet as your children now. If the police had not come, where would we all be? Bad men and whisky were killing us so fast, but the police have protected us as the feathers of the bird protect it from the frosts of winter. I am satisfied. I will sign the treaty."

And Red Crow spoke also.

"Three years ago, I first shook hands with Macleod at Old Man's River. Since that time he has made me many promises. He kept them all—not one has ever been broken. I trust him entirely, I will sign with Crowfoot."

They all said that, and finally I had to stand.

"I cannot be alone. I must say what my people say. I will sign."

And then Macleod opened his square, bearded mouth. "I am gratified to hear your kind words. I told you when I came that nothing would be taken from you without your consent, and every promise we make to you here will be kept as certainly as the sun now shines upon us."

So on Saturday, September 22, 1877, we touched the pen and "did thereby cede, release, surrender and yield up forever" fifty thousand square miles—as much land as the Queen's entire country—for five dollars per person per year and a medal and a new suit of clothing for each chief every three years. Oh, there was a great deal of eating and handshaking, and four hundred of our warriors dressed their horses as for war and charged down the hills to circle the square tents of the police, shooting and screaming their war cries. But it meant nothing.

The life we had lived since before the memories of our oldest fathers was gone. Four thousand three hundred and ninety-two of us had been paid off.

That winter three of our chiefs died. Crowfoot had to go to a white doctor to be cured of an illness. No snow fell on the prairies, and no buffalo came toward the foothills. Instead, prairie fires burned the earth black. And in two years there was not a single buffalo left on the land we had given away; in three, we had only flour "not quite unfit for food" to eat; and in four, one thousand five hundred of us were dead.

My X is on the treaty. It is there following Crowfoot and Old Sun and Bull Head and Red Crow, the fifth of fifty-one chiefs and councillors.

I knew about money then, but I did not know what the treaty meant by "reserves to allow one square mile for each family of five persons." I know now, since I have lived on this "small place, land set aside." I will live here, remembering, forever.

But there is still the land.

Looking toward the Red Deer River from the Hand Hills.

The railway winds into Carbon.

Overleaf: Evening falls across an ocean of prairie,
near Suffield.

Associate Editor / Carlotta Lemieux
Designer / David Shaw
Composition / Attic Typesetting
Film Preparation / Artcraft Engravers Ltd.
Printing / York Litho Ltd.
Binding / T. H. Best Company Ltd.